A MIDSUMMER NIGHT'S DREAM

NOTES

including
- *Life of Shakespeare*
- *Brief Summary of the Play*
- *List of Characters*
- *Summaries and Commentaries*
- *Critical Analysis*
- *Study Questions*
- *Bibliography*

by
Matthew Black, Ph.D.
University of Pennsylvania

Cliffs Notes
INCORPORATED
LINCOLN, NEBRASKA 68501

Editor	Consulting Editor
Gary Carey, M.A. *University of Colorado*	*James L. Roberts, Ph.D.* *Department of English* *University of Nebraska*

ISBN 0-8220-0057-1
© Copyright 1981
by
Cliffs Notes, Inc.
All Rights Reserved
Printed in U.S.A.

1996 Printing

Cliffs Notes, Inc.   Lincoln, Nebraska

CONTENTS

A MIDSUMMER-NIGHT'S DREAM NOTES

LIFE OF SHAKESPEARE

Many books have assembled facts, reasonable suppositions, traditions, and speculations concerning the life and career of William Shakespeare. Taken as a whole, these materials give a rather comprehensive picture of England's foremost dramatic poet. Tradition and sober supposition are not necessarily false because they lack proved bases for their existence. It is important, however, that persons interested in Shakespeare should distinguish between *facts* and *beliefs* about his life.

From one point of view, modern scholars are fortunate to know as much as they do about a man of middle-class origin who left a small English country town and embarked on a professional career in sixteenth-century London. From another point of view, they know surprisingly little about the writer who has continued to influence the English language and its drama and poetry for more than three hundred years. Sparse and scattered as these facts of his life are, they are sufficient to prove that a man from Stratford by the name of William Shakespeare wrote the major portion of the thirty-seven plays which scholars ascribe to him. The concise review which follows will concern itself with some of these records.

No one knows the exact date of William Shakespeare's birth. His baptism occurred on Wednesday, April 26, 1564. His father was John Shakespeare, tanner, glover, dealer in grain, and town official of Stratford; his mother, Mary, was the daughter of Robert Arden, a prosperous gentleman-farmer. The Shakespeares lived on Henley Street.

Under a bond dated November 28, 1582, William Shakespeare and Anne Hathaway entered into a marriage contract. The baptism of their eldest child, Susanna, took place in Stratford in May, 1583. One year and nine months later their twins, Hamnet and Judith, were christened in the same church. The parents named them for the poet's friends Hamnet and Judith Sadler.

Early in 1596, William Shakespeare, in his father's name, applied to the College of Heralds for a coat of arms. Although positive proof is lacking, there is reason to believe that the Heralds granted this request, for in 1599 Shakespeare again made application for the right to quarter his coat of arms with that of his mother. Entitled to her father's coat of arms, Mary had lost this privilege when she married John Shakespeare before he held the official status of gentleman.

In May of 1597, Shakespeare purchased New Place, the outstanding residential property in Stratford at that time. Since John Shakespeare had suffered financial reverses prior to this date, William must have achieved success for himself.

Court records show that in 1601 or 1602, William Shakespeare began rooming in the household of Christopher Mountjoy in London. Subsequent disputes between Shakespeare's landlord, Mountjoy, and his son-in-law, Stephen Belott, over Stephen's wedding settlement led to a series of legal actions, and in 1612 the court scribe recorded Shakespeare's deposition of testimony relating to the case.

In July, 1605, William Shakespeare paid four hundred and forty pounds for the lease of a large portion of the tithes on certain real estate in and near Stratford. This was an arrangement whereby Shakespeare purchased half the annual tithes, or taxes, on certain agricultural products from sections of land in and near Stratford. In addition to receiving approximately ten percent income on his investment, he almost doubled his capital. This was possibly the most important and successful investment of his lifetime, and it paid a steady income for many years.

Shakespeare is next mentioned when John Combe, a resident of Stratford, died on July 12, 1614. To his friend, Combe bequeathed the sum of five pounds. These records and similar ones are important, not because of their economic significance but because they prove the existence of a William Shakespeare in Stratford and in London during this period.

On March 25, 1616, William Shakespeare revised his last will and testament. He died on April 23 of the same year. His body lies within the chancel and before the altar of the Stratford church. A rather wry inscription is carved upon his tombstone:

Good Friend, for Jesus' sake, forbear
To dig the dust enclosed here;
Blest be the man that spares these stones
And curst be he that moves my bones.

The last direct descendant of William Shakespeare was his granddaughter, Elizabeth Hall, who died in 1670.

These are the most outstanding facts about Shakespeare the man, as apart from those about the dramatist and poet. Such pieces of information, scattered from 1564 through 1616, declare the existence of such a person, not as a writer or actor, but as a private citizen. It is illogical to think that anyone would or could have fabricated these details for the purpose of deceiving later generations.

In similar fashion, the evidence establishing William Shakespeare as the foremost playwright of his day is positive and persuasive. Robert Greene's *Groatsworth of Wit*, in which he attacked Shakespeare, a mere actor, for presuming to write plays in competition with Greene and his fellow playwrights, was entered in the *Stationers' Register* on September 20, 1592. In 1594 Shakespeare acted before Queen Elizabeth, and in 1594 and 1595 his name appeared as one of the shareholders of the Lord Chamberlain's Company. Francis Meres in his *Palladis Tamia* (1598) called Shakespeare "mellifluous and hony-tongued" and compared his comedies and tragedies with those of Plautus and Seneca in excellence.

Shakespeare's continued association with Burbage's company is equally definite. His name appears as one of the owners of the Globe in 1599. On May 19, 1603, he and his fellow actors received a patent from James I designating them as the King's Men and making them Grooms of the Chamber. Late in 1608 or early in 1609, Shakespeare and his colleagues purchased the Blackfriars Theatre and began using it as their winter location when weather made production at the Globe inconvenient.

Other specific allusions to Shakespeare, to his acting and his writing, occur in numerous places. Put together, they form irrefutable testimony that William Shakespeare of Stratford and London was the leader among Elizabethan playwrights.

One of the most impressive of all proofs of Shakespeare's authorship of his plays is the First Folio of 1623, with the dedicatory verse which appeared in it. John Heminge and Henry Condell, members of Shakespeare's own company, stated that they collected and issued the plays as a memorial to their fellow actor. Many contemporary poets contributed eulogies to Shakespeare; one of the best known of these poems is by Ben Jonson, a fellow actor and, later, a friendly rival. Jonson also criticized Shakespeare's dramatic work in *Timber: or, Discoveries* (1641).

Certainly there are many things about Shakespeare's genius and career which the most diligent scholars do not know and cannot explain, but the facts which do exist are sufficient to establish Shakespeare's identity as a man and his authorship of the thirty-seven plays which reputable critics acknowledge to be his.

BRIEF SUMMARY OF THE PLAY

The action of *A Midsummer-Night's Dream* takes place in a mythical Athens. Theseus, the reigning Duke, has conquered the Amazons and has fallen in love with their beautiful queen, Hippolyta. As the play opens, he proclaims that their wedding is to take place in five days.

At this point, Egeus, a wealthy Athenian, brings his daughter Hermia before the Duke. Having fallen in love with Lysander, a young man of whom her father disapproves, Hermia has refused to marry Demetrius, who is her father's choice. Demetrius had been in love with Hermia's friend, Helena, but had abandoned her for Hermia.

Angered by Hermia's disobedience to his will, Egeus demands judgment on his daughter. Regretfully, the Duke tells Hermia that according to Athenian law, she must marry Demetrius or die. The only other alternative is a life of chastity as a virgin priestess. She has until the Duke's wedding day to decide.

After the others leave, Hermia and Lysander determine to meet in a wood near the city the following night. Then they plan to leave the city and go to a place outside of Athenian jurisdiction where they can be married. Helena promises to help the lovers, and they leave. When Demetrius returns, Helena, who is hopelessly in love with him, tries to win his favor by telling him of Hermia's plan to elope. She is bitterly disappointed when Demetrius hurries away to stop the elopement, but she follows him.

In another part of Athens, a group of common laboring men, led by Peter Quince, a carpenter, are preparing a play to be given at the wedding feast of Theseus and Hippolyta. The "star" of the group, Nick Bottom, a weaver, struts and boasts of his ability to play any and all parts and is finally cast as the hero in a "most lamentable comedy" about "the most cruel death of Pyramus and Thisby." All the parts are assigned and the rehearsal is set to take place the next night in the wood outside of Athens—the same wood in which Hermia and Lysander are to meet.

The night in question is Midsummer's Eve, a time of great rejoicing and mischief among the fairies who live in the wood. Oberon, their King, and Titania, their Queen, have quarreled over possession of a little boy, the child of one of Titania's priestesses. To resolve the quarrel, humble his proud Queen, and gain the boy for his own group of followers, Oberon enlists the aid of Puck (Robin Goodfellow). This clever and mischievous fairy delights in playing tricks on mortals and is a faithful servant of Oberon.

By putting the nectar of a magic flower on the eyes of the sleeping Lysander, Puck causes him to fall in love with Helena and forsake Hermia. Into this confusion come Bottom and his amateur acting troupe. Puck turns Bottom's head into the head of an ass, frightening off all his friends and leaving the weaver alone. He comes upon Titania, the Queen of the Fairies, and awakens her from her sleep. Her eyes, like those of Lysander, have been anointed with the magic nectar, and she falls in love with the first creature she sees. Her new love is, of course, Bottom—with his ass's head.

After playing various pranks on Titania, Bottom, and the two pairs of lovers, Oberon relents and has Puck set things right again. Lysander and Hermia are reunited, and Demetrius, with the aid of the magic juice, rediscovers his love for Helena. Titania and Bottom are released from their enchantments, and she agrees to give Oberon the little boy about whom they had quarrelled.

Unsure whether what occurred was fact or nightmare, the lovers come upon the Duke and his party hunting in the woods that morning. After hearing their stories, he proclaims that to his wedding will be added those of the four young lovers.

Bottom awakens, is confused, but returns to Athens and, with his friends, prepares to give their play at the Duke's wedding.

After the triple wedding, the play, "Pyramus and Thisby," is presented as part of the entertainment. It is performed so earnestly and so badly that the assembled guests are weak from laughter. After the performance, the newlyweds adjourn to bed, and the fairies appear to confer a final blessing on the happy couples.

LIST OF CHARACTERS

Theseus

Duke of Athens; although his part is brief, it is commanding. He represents authority in the play, but because the play is a comedy, we laugh at his eagerness to be wedded and bedded as quickly as possible. Shakespeare has keenly combined a sense of Theseus' splendid and gracious aristocracy with his mortal, agitated urgency for sexual enjoyment.

Egeus

Father to Hermia; a domineering and overbearing man who insists that his daughter marry the man whom he has chosen for her. We have little sympathy or no sympathy for him since he would have his daughter put to death rather than marry a man whom he thoroughly disapproves of. Egeus represents the epitome of the stern, uncompromising letter-of-the-law type of Athenian justice.

Lysander

Beloved of Hermia, Lysander, Egeus believes, cannot be trusted as a suitor for his daughter. He believes that Lysander feigns love and is not of the proper social "status" for Hermia; on the contrary, Lysander is and, what is more, he loves her deeply, is a romantic, and yet is also a realist for it is he who says, "The course of true love never did run smooth. . . ." In addition, he says that love is "swift as a shadow, [and] short as any dream," and he speaks of the "jaws of darkness" threatening love. These are not the words of a man who is only momentarily infatuated with Hermia.

Demetrius

Suitor to Hermia with the consent of Egeus, he is certainly not a "model" lover, by any means. Pursued by Helena, he is finally ready to abandon her to the "mercy of wild beasts." Yet when Demetrius' eyes are "opened," he returns to the woman he once loved, Helena. In all, he is a fanciful man, fond of punning; one should not take his romantic irrationalities too seriously.

Philostrate

Master of the Revels to Theseus, he seems to serve very little purpose other than arrange for the wedding entertainment. His sole distinguishing feature, perhaps, is his scorn of the players; the performance, he feels, is too ridiculous for royalty.

Hippolyta

Queen of the Amazons, betrothed to Theseus. It is difficult to imagine that this woman was once a war-like creature. Now tamed by her lover, she abides by his every word. Her love for Theseus represents a kind of framework of rational love in this play which is laced throughout with fanciful, sentimental, and often artificial passion and avowals of love.

Hermia

Daughter to Egeus, in love with Lysander. She is a tiny young woman of dark complexion. For this, she is mocked, but even Helena speaks of her sparkling eyes and lovely voice. She is ultimately charming, despite her spirited and independent temper. Her deep love for Lysander has made her a vixen—in the viewpoint of her father, but she has a soft, teasing side to her strident, quick-tempered spirit.

Helena

In love with Demetrius, she is a tall, lovely young blonde woman. Superficially, one might guess that she is passive, but she is not. Her "gentle" love for Demetrius is fierce and fiery. No one can dissuade her that her love for him is hopeless—and as it turns out, the two young people are finally united in marriage.

Oberon

King of the Fairies. We assume that he must be very diminutive, and we know that he can make himself invisible. Like Puck, his jester, he can sail around the globe in minutes, but he is not a mere fleet-winged fairy. His moods are deeply mortal; he is envious, capable of revenge, and great anger. He will stop at nothing to get what he wants. Here, it is the little Indian boy, who is a member of Titania's attendants. By means of magic, he attains the boy.

Titania

Queen of the Fairies, she is most concerned with beauty, sweetness, and pleasantness—if possible (Oberon is a constant test of her good nature). She adores lovely things and is deeply loyal to all her subjects, especially to the memory of the Indian boy's mother. Her bewitched "love" for Bottom shows that her ability to offer devotion to him is boundless. She has a natural charm that makes her, even in her comic affection for the ass-headed Bottom, one of the most lovely "women" Shakespeare ever created.

Puck, or Robin Goodfellow

Oberon's jester is never still a moment. He is the spirit of mischief and irresponsibility. Like Oberon, he is a tiny creature, and he prides himself on how quickly he can circle the globe. He is capable of good deeds, but he prefers to play practical jokes. Love is a joke to him, as are mortals in love, but, ironically, we cannot help but love Puck. Shakespeare created an imp who is able to laugh at all woes and see the transitory nature of emotion; he embodied within this creature some of his most exquisite, memorable lines of philosophical shrewdness.

Peter Quince

A carpenter; author of "Pyramus and Thisby." His most remarkable virtue is his patience. His friend Bottom's irrepressible, nervous energy would try a saint's tolerance. Quince also deals capably with Bottom.

Nick Bottom

A weaver; "Pyramus." More than any of the other characters in the play, Bottom is the best realized. Humor and good nature exude from him. He is an impromptu master of wit, but he carries his talents for the ridiculous to such extremes that he often seems to be an "ass"—which is why the ass's head that Puck transforms upon him is so very apropos. Bottom's humor, his extravagance, his malapropisms, and his unabashed delight in life have made him one of Shakespeare's favorite characters.

Francis Flute

A bellows-maker; "Thisby." Despite his tiny, rather effeminate body, he does not want to be the heroine of Quince's play. He performs well, however; and it is he, more than any of the other artisans, who idolizes Bottom as a consummate actor and human being.

Tom Snout

A tinker; a "Wall." Besides being the Wall, he is probably the most visually comic figure in the play, for he is roughly plastered with mortar and stones throughout the wedding entertainment.

Snug

A joiner; "Lion." We never know Snug's given name. Possibly, even he does not remember it, for when he was assigned the part of the Lion, a part which requires no more talent than roaring, he is afraid that he cannot remember his lines.

Robin Starveling

A tailor; "Moonshine." Like Snout (the Wall), he is very shy, and he attempts to explain to the audience who he is; he forgets his lines and he exhausts Hippolyta's patience.

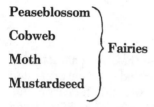

Peaseblossom
Cobweb
Moth
Mustardseed
} Fairies

SUMMARIES AND COMMENTARIES

ACT I—SCENE 1

Summary

The play opens in the royal palace of ancient Athens. Theseus, Athens' famous and popular ruler, is anxious for the rising of the new moon on May Day, when he will be married to Hippolyta, Queen of the Amazons. He orders Philostrate, his Master of the Revels, to devise entertainments that will while away the time and distract his impatience.

An unexpected diversion is provided, however, by the entrance of Egeus, an angry father who lays before the Duke a marriage problem. Egeus' daughter Hermia, small, dark, and spirited, is being wooed by two youths, Lysander and Demetrius. Egeus wishes his daughter to marry Demetrius and complains that Lysander has stolen her heart with poems, serenades, and "sweetmeats." Athenian law, Egeus says and Theseus confirms, decrees that she must wed her father's choice of a husband or die. The only alternative which Theseus can offer is that she become a nun. Hermia, undaunted, says that she *will* marry the man she loves or die unwed. Lysander argues that he is the equal of Demetrius in status and wealth; also, he loves Hermia more than Demetrius does, and, best of all, he is beloved by her. Moreover, he tells Theseus how Demetrius wooed and won and then jilted Helena; in other words, Egeus' choice of a future son-in-law is a cad. None of the disputants will yield an inch. Theseus repeats the choices which Hermia has: if she insists on marrying Lysander, she is doomed to die or else she can become a nun. Theseus then leaves, taking Hippolyta, Egeus, and Demetrius with him, and leaving Hermia and Lysander alone.

Lysander proposes that they elope to the house of a rich aunt of his who lives outside the jurisdiction of Athenian law, and Hermia gladly agrees, promising to meet him that night in a wood some miles from Athens. Just then Helena appears. She is Hermia's dearest friend, but very different from her; she is tall and blonde—and timid. She pleads with Hermia to tell her how to win Demetrius, and Hermia and Lysander comfort her by telling her of their plan to elope. When this is accomplished, Demetrius will no longer pursue Hermia and perhaps he will return to Helena. After they have gone, Helena, still grieving over Demetrius' former attention and his present indifference, decides to tell him of the elopement so that, at least, she can go with him in pursuit of the lovers.

Commentary

Basically, this first scene introduces us to two sets of the lovers: Theseus and Hippolyta, and Hermia and Lysander. But Shakespeare complicates the situation by introducing Demetrius, who loves Hermia, and Helena who loves Demetrius. After this first scene, the royal lovers, Theseus and Hippolyta, will step aside from the action and will allow the untitled lovers to dominate the action. Logically, one might expect this play to concern itself with the royal personages, with the love affairs of the citizens being the subplot, but since this is a comedy, the situation is reversed, and it focuses, instead, on the common man and, here in particular, the common *woman*, and the ecstasies of love.

As a setting for his comedy, Shakespeare chose a long-ago mythical era in ancient Greece. Since the audience would probably be somewhat familiar with the notion that Greek gods and goddesses might do the unexpected, it gave him considerable opportunity to use the surprising and amusing mischief of the fairy kingdom.

According to scholars, this comedy was written to be performed at a wedding of noble persons on a private estate, where Queen Elizabeth herself is believed to have been present. (Their evidence for this is contained in the lofty and copious compliments offered to her in Act I, Scene I, 74-75.) Accordingly, this play has a light-hearted attitude throughout, despite the elaborate confusion of lovers and their sighs, tears, and passionate avowals. One should sit back, relax, and imagine the gossamer and moonlight that Shakespeare suggests in order to show us that dreams are usually best forgotten, but fantasy—especially love's fantasy—is necessary for a basic understanding of human relationships.

Since this play was written strictly for entertainment, the development and delineation of characters are not nearly as detailed or as in depth as they are in Shakespeare's tragedies. The play concerns love and passion, but it deals primarily with the comical complications of love. Consequently, all that one need do, initially, is try and remember who loves whom and enjoy this tale of gaiety, magic, and mismatched lovers.

In this kingdom of ancient Athens, a man's word is law—whether it is the word of Theseus, the Duke of Athens, or that of Egeus, the father of the unhappy Hermia. Egeus is so furious with his daughter that he is ready to have her condemned to death for disobeying him. Hermia, one should note, is very lucky that her case is pleaded before a young ruler who is himself very much in love and anxious to be wed. An old, misanthropic curmudgeon would have silenced Hermia's passionate challenges in a minute. Theseus, in contrast, tempers Athen's harsh laws and offers Hermia an alternative to the death or chastity that she self-imposes upon herself. He does so, however, only half-heartedly, for even he cannot find much consolation in prescribing a nun's life for this young woman. The idea of being forever chaste is unappealing to him. Even an unhappy marriage, he tells Hermia, is preferable to "chanting faint hymns to the cold fruitless moon." Love's passion, however, is at stake for Hermia, and she refuses to compromise her virginity to her father's choice of a husband. She will not accept any "unwished yoke," and her "soul consents not to give sovereignty" to anyone but her own heart.

Hermia, in fact, seems far more spirited than Theseus' fiancee, Hippolyta, queen and leader of the Amazons. Now that Theseus and his men have defeated Hippolyta and her warrior-women, she is only a faint shadow of her former self. Only once does she speak during this scene; she seems absolutely to have accepted Theseus' conquest of her. It seems hardly possible that she was once boldly self-assertive and militant; now she poetically demurs to Theseus' presence. Her passivity, in contrast to Hermia's spirit, makes the young girl's passionate agony even more pressing and immediate.

One of the best ways to judge and evaluate a dramatic character is to see that character in action with a variety of persons and note the variations and changes in temperament and attitude. This we are able to do when Hermia is left alone with Lysander, and her best friend, Helena, enters. Dramatically, Helena is a foil for Hermia—that is, she is someone who is strongly contrasted with her and who will be a counterpoint to enhance Hermia's distinctive characteristics. What is more, Helena was once the beloved of Demetrius and if she can win back his love, then Hermia and Lysander will be free to wed. So the plot hangs heavily on Helena's success in recapturing Demetrius' favor, and in this scene she decides that it is in her best interests to tell Demetrius of Hermia and Lysander's secret plan to elope. She is willing to risk his following the lovers, if only she can accompany him on the pursuit. Like Hermia, Helena is a victim of love, but in her case, she is a victim of Demetrius' inconstancy; Hermia is a victim of Athen's unjust laws. Unlike Hermia, Helena (according to Lysander) "dotes,/Devoutly dotes, dotes in idolatry." He suggests that Helena is less serious than Hermia. Hermia champions her own cause, while Helena is content to trust fate, following Demetrius blindly, and hoping that when he sees the lovers elope, he will return to her arms.

We should also note the change in temperament and attitude of Hermia during her moments with Lysander. Her mood changes: she seems emotionally drained; she is no longer the angry and frustrated daughter. The dramatic transformation is exaggerated, of course, to produce a comic effect. With her beloved Lysander, she becomes much more like Hippolyta, hopelessly in love. She is so inordinately overcome that she refers to the tears that well in her eyes as being a "tempest" that could perhaps revive the faded roses in her cheeks. It is at this point that Lysander offers a comment which has been uttered by wise men and lovers ever since: "The course of true love never did run smooth." To which Hermia's anguished soul cries out,

"O cross! . . . O spite . . . O hell!" She is a victim of one of life's cruelest dilemmas—a difference in her choice of a lover and her father's choice. Hermia is a victim of fate's caprice, of "an edict in destiny." These calamities, then, are not merely Hermia's and Lysander's problems. They have plagued lovers since time immemorial, and so the crushing problems of these lovers give the scene a universality which the audience can easily sympathize with.

ACT I—SCENE 2

Summary

That same day, at the house of the carpenter Peter Quince, a company of amateur actors is preparing an interlude, or short comic play, to be performed before Theseus and Hippolyta in the evening after their marriage. The purpose of the meeting is for Quince, the host and director, to cast the actors, give out the parts, and set the time for a rehearsal. But everything Quince proposes meets with some objection. The chief difficulty is a bumptious fellow named Nick Bottom, a weaver, who tries to run the meeting. Quince humors him by explaining that their play is to be about Pyramus and Thisby; in the tragic legend, the two young and beautiful lovers' families lived next door to one another in ancient Babylon. They stole out to meet, just as Hermia and Lysander plan to do, and died by their own hands in a misadventure involving a lion. Quince does not need to go into this in much detail since many people in Shakespeare's audience would know the story; Quince does describe it, though, as a "most lamentable comedy," as indeed its performance at court turns out to be.

Bottom asks what part he is to play. Pyramus, a lover, Quince tells him. Bottom assures them all that he will be a most mournful lover and will make the audience weep. Still, he wishes that he could play a tyrant, and he proclaims some "lofty" verse to show how he would rant if he were cast as a tyrant. Quince ignores him and next casts a fellow named Flute as the heroine, Thisby. Bottom says that he, Bottom, could also play a girl, and he speaks a line or two in falsetto to show his versatility. Quince ignores him and assigns the other parts until he comes to the part of the Lion, which he wants to be *roared* by Snug. Snug asks if Quince has the Lion's part written out (remember, it is nothing but roaring). Snug says that he is a slow memorizer; he might not be able to do justice to the role. Bottom is alert and realizes that here is one more chance for him to play yet another role—the Lion! And he shows how well he can roar. But Quince flatters him into being content with the leading role and then gives out the written parts and sets a rehearsal for that night in the very wood where Lysander and Hermia plan to meet. The company is then dismissed by Bottom, who by this time has taken over the role of director. All of this is done in "deadpan"; Quince and his friends have absolutely no doubts about the sterling excellence of the play which they plan to perform or about their ability to enact it.

Commentary

It is indeed a motley lot that makes up the characters of this scene. Presumably, Philostrate, Theseus' Master of the Revels, has rounded up these fellows to devise suitable entertainment for Theseus and Hippolyta's wedding. These bumpkins, however, are a far cry from the "Athenian youth" that Theseus requested. Here we have a carpenter, a weaver, a joiner, a bellows-maker, a tinker, and a tailor, all functioning as the broad comedy relief within the framework of Shakespeare's light romantic comedy. Their names, one might note, are fitted to their trades: Quince, whose name suggests "quoins," or wedges, is a carpenter; Snug is a joiner, or cabinet-maker, who makes "snug" joints; Bottom is a weaver and named for the "bottom" or reel on which thread is wound; Flute the bellows-maker has a name which suggests one of the pipes of a church organ, an instrument which was supplied with air by a hand-pumped bellows; in addition, he has a flute-like voice which is well suited for the role of a girl, which he will be asked to perform in the nuptial play; Snout the tinker probably mends the spouts of kettles; and as for Starveling the tailor, tailors were proverbially thin, and in the words of an Elizabethan jingle, it took nine narrow tailors to make one husky man. The incongruity of these tradesmen fashioning a suitable interlude of entertainment quickly sets the tone for this raucous scene and for the upcoming slapstick entertainment.

Quince, because this scene is set at his house, assumes the role of director for this interlude, or play-within-a-play. It will be performed on "the next new moon" and will be performed at night. As a coincidence, the magical antics performed by the fairies upon Hermia, Lysander, Helena, and Demetrius will also be performed at night. When the audience learns the title of the play which Quince has chosen, the situation is ready-made for laughter: "The Most Lamentable Comedy and Most Cruel Death of Pyramus and Thisby." In addition to the incongruity of the rustic tradesmen devising appropriately regal entertainment for Athens' upcoming royal wedding, this play that they plan to perform is a "lamentable comedy"—a dramatic vehicle contrary to all reason and propriety. The choice is, without question, certainly lamentable; a wedding is a time for gaiety and pleasure. One does *not* stage a dramatic piece that deals with dying lovers as entertainment for wedding nuptials. This bad taste is the height of absurdity, as is Quince's deep seriousness about the excellent production of the play and about these tradesmen being "best fit" to perform.

Of equally comic seriousness is Bottom the weaver. His first lines establish him as an enthusiastic organizer, ready and willing to take charge. He catches our attention immediately by presuming to direct Quince. Bottom is irrepressible, a natural ham, eager to volunteer his services for every role in the play. We sense that the rest of the tradesmen like him and respect him, however. Note, for instance, that when he interrupts to add a word of advice or a suggestion, which is frequently, the company is impressed. As an example, Bottom is absolutely convinced that the "lamentable" piece dealing with the deaths of two lovers is "a very good piece of work" and, in addition, that it is a "merry" one. Moments later, we realize that Bottom has absolutely no idea what the play is about. When Quince casts Bottom as the lead (Pyramus), Bottom eagerly accepts the role, but asks, "What is Pyramus? a lover, or a tyrant?" Besides exposing Bottom's ignorance of the plot, the situation causes the audience to chuckle at the unexpected juxtaposition of lover and tyrant. These are not diametrical opposites, however, as the simple Bottom might suppose. One can love and be a tyrant. We have just seen a situation in which Egeus loves his daughter, but at the same time he is certainly a tyrant when he tries to force Hermia to marry a man she does not love. In fact, he would have her condemned to death for disobeying his command. Even Theseus himself was a tyrant of sorts when he comandeered his army to success and was able to love Hippolyta only after he conquered her.

When Quince replies that Pyramus is defined as a lover who kills himself for love, we recall a parallel situation in Scene 1. Hermia loves Lysander so much that if she cannot have him, she is willing to submit to the law of Athens that would demand her life. Furthermore, Quince has some fun with Bottom when he tells him that Pyramus kills himself "most gallant." The phrase is set off from the rest of Quince's speech by commas, and in the comic context, it almost demands that Quince clasp one hand to his heart and another to his forehead as he indulges in Bottom's grandiloquent flair for acting.

Lover or tyrant, Bottom is self-confident that he can perform more than adequately. And he launches into vocal proof. His mini-soliloquy awes the rest of the sextet which Quince has assembled. It has a hard-hitting beat, its rhymes resound boldly, and the language is sufficiently literary and vague to "sound good." As Bottom says, "This was lofty." But note that even now he does not stop. He continues to mutter afterthoughts on both tyrants and lovers. Bottom himself is a bit of a gentle tyrant here, dominating stage-center, confident that as long as *he* plays the dramatic lead and ponders sufficiently on its interpretation, the play will be a smashing success.

The part of Thisby is given to Francis Flute, and there is much humor laced through Flute's brief reply. Flute, like most men, would prefer to play a manly role, perhaps that of a romantic bachelor-knight; he does *not* want to play a woman's role. Although young men and boys regularly acted women's roles in Elizabethan dramas, there was sufficient joking and puns about this dramatic convention that we can understand Flute's objections to donning a skirt. Flute protests that he cannot play Thisby because he has a beard "coming"; in other words, his face is currently virgin smooth. His argument is not sufficiently convincing for Quince; if his "coming" beard suddenly appears full-bushed, then Flute shall play the role of Thisby with a mask.

At this point, we are not really surprised when Bottom breaks into a falsetto and offers, in a "monstrous little voice," to demonstrate another of his dramatic talents by playing Thisby, too. As one might guess, the role of Bottom is an actor's delight, just as Bottom believes himself to be a natural for the audience's delight.

Like Flute's reluctance to perform his assigned role, Snug the cabinet maker has misgivings about *his* role and offers Bottom another chance for yet another role when he fears that he will *not* be a quick study for the lion's role. Vocally, it must be admitted, Bottom has an amazing range—from the lofty voiced tyrant, to the shrill voiced maiden, to the non-pareiled roaring lion who will, Bottom promises, move Theseus to call for successive encores of roaring: "Let him roar again; let him roar again." Wisely, Quince quiets his leonine crony—almost, for Bottom announces that if, possibly, he would roar too loudly for the gentle Hippolyta, then he will roar as "gently as any sucking dove." Clearly, Bottom's thespian talents are bottomless. The scene ends with plans made to rehearse tomorrow night "in the palace wood . . . by moonlight," with Bottom promising to rehearse "most obscenely" (another of his amusing malapropisms) and advising the others to be there or "cut bowstrings," a variation on the Midwestern phrase, "either fish (seriously) or cut bait"; in other words, No Nonsense!—which is *exactly* what we have just listened to in this entire scene.

ACT II—SCENE 1

Summary

As the curtains open on this act, the fairies, traditionally active on Midsummer's Eve, come flitting before us. One of them encounters Robin Goodfellow, or Puck (a mischievous elf), and tells him that Titania, the Fairy Queen, and her court are due any minute in this wooded glade. Puck warns her that Oberon, the Fairy King, also intends to use the place for *his* revels, and that Oberon is furious with Titania over a young boy whom she stole in India (the home of the fairy kingdom). Oberon wants this boy to be his "henchman" (chief page) for his band of fairies. If Oberon and Titania meet, says Puck, there will be a fierce quarrel. At that moment, the fairy recognizes Robin as the infamous Puck, who plays tricks on mortals in order to make his master, Oberon, laugh. Puck admits that he is indeed the famed fairy, and he recounts with much boasting some of the many and varied tricks he has played. It is he who skims the milk set out for cream, curdles the milk in the churn, and spoils the butter making, in addition to making old ladies spill cider on their withered throats. He especially likes to neigh like a filly to torment stallions.

Suddenly Oberon with his court enters—just as Titania with her court enters from the opposite direction. And as Puck predicted, they quarrel at once. Titania chides Oberon for his lengthy devotion to Hippolyta and insists that his over-concern for the "bouncing Amazon" and her forthcoming marriage has brought him "from the farthest steep of India." Oberon counters by accusing Titania of loving Theseus and inducing him to jilt several mistresses. Titania retorts that these are jealous lies and rumors, and she blames Oberon's persecution of her for the recent storms and floods, the rotting crops, and the plague of "rheumatic diseases" on earth. Oberon replies that, on the contrary, that it is *she* who is responsible; he says that if she will let him have the Indian boy for his retinue, all the troubles which the mortals are suffering will cease. "Not for thy kingdom," Titania vows, and she and her court depart.

Oberon plots revenge. He tells Puck about a night when he saw a strange and wonderful sight: Cupid, with his bow taut and an arrow cocked, was flying between earth and the moon; he released the arrow toward a beautiful mortal virgin, but the arrow missed her heart. As it fell to earth, it struck a milk-white pansy and turned it purple with desire. From that time on, the flower was magical; that is, if the nectar of a pansy is dropped onto the eyelids of a sleeper, mortal or fairy, it will make him, or her, fall in love with the first living creature seen upon waking. "Fetch me that flower," Oberon commands. Puck boasts that he can do it and, what's more, he can circle the globe in forty minutes. Oberon's plan is to squeeze a globule of pansy nectar onto Titania's eyelids while she is sleeping so that when she wakes she will dote on the first living thing she sees. Later, by offering to remove the spell, which he can do by means of another herb, he can blackmail her into giving him the Indian boy.

While Oberon is scheming, Demetrius, with Helena in hot pursuit, runs into the wooded glade. They do not see Oberon (he has just told us that he has used his power to become invisible). Helena's desire is to win Demetrius; his is to kill Lysander, recover Hermia, and lose Helena in the woods. Eluding Helena, however, is difficult for she loves him so much that neither his reasoning, scorn, or threats (nor her own modesty) can rout her. In desperation, Demetrius races out with Helena following and vowing to win him.

Oberon, who has overheard their quarrel, decides impulsively that he will reverse Helena's and Demetrius' personalities; shortly, it will be *Helena* who will be fleeing from *Demetrius*. Just then, Puck returns with a pansy, which Oberon plans to use on Titania. But before he leaves, he gives some of the nectar to Puck, ordering him to anoint the eyes of a young Athenian lad who will be sleeping in these woods; if Puck does so, the fellow will fall in love with the woman whom he now scorns. Puck promises to do what Oberon requests.

Commentary

For this play, it is essential that our imaginations must believe in what was known in Elizabethan times as "midsummer madness," a time when fairies were everywhere and magic was powerful. Shakespeare's audience believed that on the eve of May 1st, all sorts of supernatural happenings might occur. Early in the act, one of the fairies describes for Puck (but, more important, for us) exactly *who* he is and how he cavorts "over hill, over dale," etc. He mentions the fact that he is able to go "everywhere. . . . [He is] swifter than the moon's sphere" (6-7). His magical fairy characteristics are clear. Even today, there exists a remnant of this belief in the supernatural when children hang Maybaskets on neighbors' doors and ring the bell, making it seem as if the flowers appeared magically.

Magic is the key, then, to this play, and the fantasy that occurs is due largely to the magic of the *moon*. In this scene, the actors make several references to it, insuring that the audience is always aware of its presence. Shakespeare sustains throughout the scene a sense that the stage is being bathed in moonlight and the magic which they see is caused by the magical properties of the moon.

Shakespeare was taking a dramatic gamble when he introduced fairies onto the stage. These are no mere will o'the wisps of childrens' lore that contribute only to the play's atmosphere. These fairies have three-dimensional personalities and are responsible for most of the humor and mischief that surrounds the mismatched lovers and the mistaken identities; the audience must, for the play's duration, *believe* in them. For that reason, perhaps, Shakespeare introduces us to Oberon and Titania when their emotional tempers are high, and both of them are resolved to have their own way. No compromise seems possible. In fact, these two creatures are far more human and interesting than the palid Theseus and Hippolyta; in fact, Oberon and Titania are far more dramatically dimensional than the witches in *Macbeth* or the ghost in *Hamlet*. Oberon has the full range of human emotions; he is stubborn and has a lusty, romantic nature. Besides accusing him of being enamored of the "bouncing Amazon," Hippolyta, Titania also accuses him of recently changing into a shepherd and piping pastoral love songs to a country maiden. She characterizes his jealousy as being so potent that he has caused the winds to "sow contagious fogs" and has swollen rivers until they devastated the land. All for spite, she says. Likewise, Titania is no cliché of dainty goodness. She has a sharp tongue and a possessive vehemence. Marriage has not tamed her as has, in contrast, the promise of marriage tamed Hippolyta.

This marital strife is central to Shakespeare's comic purpose. He has introduced us to a number of amorous lovers, all of whom desperately hope to be married and live happily ever after. Yet here is a married couple who argues and screams and obstinately refuses to make peace with one another. Moreover, this married couple is more than merely mortal; these are fairies, superior beings, supposedly a little less than angels. One doesn't think of fairies as being loutish and shrewish; yet they are here, and their quarreling is so intense that it is responsible for the terrible winter weather and the rheumatic diseases that mortals must suffer. Shakespeare has turned the notion of fairy-like tranquility and the ideal of love and marriage upside down. By using a humorous framework, within the confines of the fairy kingdom, he threads a vein of seriousness throughout his comedy and reminds his audience that love's perfection is a necessary illusion, for always attendant to it are a multitude of problems.

If we can believe Titania, her reason for insisting that she, and not Oberon, should keep the Indian boy is admirable. She was a good friend of the boy's mother, a mortal who was a "vot'ress," a member of a sect that honored Titania. In addition, the woman had "taken vows." It would seem that she was a virgin who became pregnant and then made Titania her confidante. Together, the two would sit on the seashore and watch the ships at sea. (In a lovely metaphor, Titania describes the woman growing "big-bellied," like the billowing sails they watched.) This woman was exceedingly generous to the fairy queen, and when she died during childbirth, Titania took her baby to rear. Titania's love for the boy is so strong, she says, that she will not give him up—even for Oberon's kingdom. Whether this is an exaggeration or not, we cannot be sure, but it makes Titania seem a little less obstinate than her husband. Ultimately, the women in this play emerge as far more honorable characters than the men. Titania even invites Oberon to join her and her court in their reveling tonight *if* he will hold his tongue and "patiently dance." Oberon stubbornly insists on having the boy, however, and so Titania and her fairies take wing and depart.

Everyone in the play is coming to these woods tonight for peace and quiet and happiness—and privacy. This is not to be the case, however; obviously the woods will be a chaos of anguished lovers, joined by the village bumpkins' mock love-heroics, and—most important—the woods will be the center of a fairy feud. Yet there is still more. Oberon plans to use his magical nectar for selfish ends and entrusts the potion to his jester Puck, mischievously telling him to also use a drop of the nectar on the eyes of the sleeping Demetrius so as to aid the mournful Helena. This is the heart of the play's whimsy—magic, which will soon become gentle madness.

ACT II—SCENE 2

Summary

In another part of the wood, Titania sends her fairy subjects off to sing while they attend to their business of curing the wild roses of cankers, killing bats to use their wings for coats, and frightening owls away. As they sing charms to keep their Queen safe from beetles, hedgehogs, newts, and snakes, she falls asleep. The fairies then fly away, leaving one of their number to guard the Queen and instructing him to stand at some distance from the royal bower. Hence, Oberon is able to approach unseen and squeeze the pansy nectar upon Titania's eyelids, at the same time pronouncing a spell which will cause her to awaken when "some vile thing is near."

As Oberon leaves, Lysander and Hermia enter, weary and tired. Titania is invisible to them. The two lovers have lost their way, and they sink to the grass and decide to rest until dawn. But a question of propriety arises. Since they are engaged, Lysander feels that they can sleep side by side in perfect innocence. But Hermia asks him to lie farther off—though not too far. Lysander obeys, and they fall asleep. Puck comes in, looking for the young Athenian man whom Oberon told him about, one who would have a girl with him. Naturally he mistakes this couple for Demetrius and Helena, whom he has never seen and who are still dashing about the forest. Seeing Lysander asleep some distance from Hermia, Puck interprets this as a sign of the disdain which Oberon described to him. So he anoints Lysander's eyes and speeds away.

A moment later, Demetrius and Helena enter the glade, still running. Demetrius, even more disdainful than before, dashes off at once, and Helena, weary and depressed, is at a loss—until she spies Lysander sleeping. She wakens him, and with his now enchanted eyes, Lysander springs up and greets her lovingly. He demands to know where Demetrius is so that he can slay him. Puzzled, Helena tries to calm Lysander by assuring him that Hermia still loves him. Describing Hermia as dull and unbeautiful, Lysander protests that he has abandoned her, and he declares that his real love is Helena. Thinking that he is mocking her, Helena runs away. Lysander, looks down at the still-sleeping Hermia and wonders how he could ever have loved her; the very sight of her makes him sick. Then off he goes in pursuit of Helena.

Hermia then awakens; she has been dreaming about a snake which crawled upon her breast, and she cries out in surprise and fear at not seeing Lysander. Terrified, she hurries off to find her beloved Lysander.

Commentary

In Oberon's last speech in the previous scene, there is a line that has become much quoted; it is wistful and romantic. Oberon, speaking of the place where he knows that he will find the sleeping Titania, says, "I know a bank where the wild thyme grows. . . ." Here, in this scene, we see the "bank where the wild thyme grows." This is the setting for the magic that Puck will produce throughout the rest of the play. It is a lovely scene that Shakespeare describes in various speeches, and one of the most beautiful moments in the scene occurs just before the Queen of the Fairies prepares for her sleep. She sends her attendants off to do their fairy duties: to kill the cankers in the rose buds (so that beauty may blossom), to do battle with bats and capture their "leathern wings" so that the tiny fairies might make themselves invincible coats against "the clamorous owl." Then to add an extra measure of exquisite enchantment to this fairy bower, the Queen's attendants sing a lullaby; when they are finished, they vanish, and Titania lies sleeping amidst the colorful "oxlips," the "nodding violets," and under a canopy of muskroses and woodbine (honeysuckle).

Oberon, as we see, was correct in his assertion that he knew exactly where Titania would be sleeping. Into this bower of peaceful beauty, he slips and squeezes the liquid from the magic flower upon Titania's eyelids. Just a few minutes earlier, the fairies had encircled their Queen and had sung a chant-song to charm away all evil creatures. The magical charms were not powerful enough, however. Now the King of the Fairies violates this pastoral setting intent on cruel mischief. Truly Oberon is far more dangerous here than the "spotted snakes" or "thorny hedgehogs" that the Queen's attendants feared might violate their mistress.

Now in a chant that is a counterpoint to the lullaby-chant that invoked protection for Titania, we hear Oberon intoning a curse upon Titania. In particular, he hopes that she sees first, on awakening, a lynx or a bear or a "bristled" boar, for he dooms her to "love and languish" for the first creature she sees. But Oberon is not even content with the idea of his Queen falling in love with a bristled boar. He hopes, finally, in a last-minute thought that "some vile thing" awakens her. He is reveling in his fiendish plot to enchant her and steal the little Indian boy. This is effective dramatically, for as he exits, we are left *not* with the idea of a boar or a lynx coming on stage. Now something else, something unknown, "some vile thing" has been promised as Titania's lover. The mystery and suspense of Oberon's curse is a masterful exit line.

When Lysander and Hermia enter this glade "where the wild thyme grows," they are speaking soft words of love to one another— a dramatic change from the dark curse of the devilish Oberon who has just left the stage. Now the problems of the fairy kingdom seem just that—ethereal problems, compared to the plight of these young mortal lovers. Recall that they have been hastening on their "seven-league" journey to Lysander's aunt's house. Now they are lost, and

Lysander confesses that he honestly has forgotten the way. His innocence is appealing. There is no bravado nor bluff about him. He is lost—and in a parallel, metaphysical sense, he is "lost"—in love. He is so innocently naive, for example, in this scene he can see no harm in his and Hermia's sharing a single "turf" for their pillow for the night. After all, he reasons, they are engaged and, as he says, "one heart, one bed, two bosoms and one troth." He is a true Romantic, in contrast to the earthy, realistic Hermia. She does not trust either his emotions or her own, and so she tells him to sleep "farther off." Nor is she impressed with his impassioned discourse on the magic of love being able to "knit two hearts into one" or his poetics about "two bosoms being interchained." He ends his protestings with one last triple-punning plea to lie beside her for the night, but Hermia will have none of his lover's posturings. She tells him that he "riddles very prettily," but to no avail: he has to sleep "farther off."

Dramatically, the audience can laugh at this gentle "lover's quibble," but the result of Hermia's demanding that Lysander sleep "farther off" will be temporarily, if comically, tragic for the young lovers. Lysander's sleeping at a distance from Hermia will be evidence for Puck that he has truly found the Athenian youth that Oberon told him about, the one who is being hounded by a woman desperately in love with him, but a woman whom he cannot stand. Visually, Puck sees a sleeping man who seemingly disdains this woman who lies "farther off." To Puck, it looks as though the woman so loves the Athenian lad that she has crept up as close as she dares so that she might imaginatively, vicariously lie beside him through the night. This piques Puck; Hermia looks like a "pretty soul." He can't understand why anyone would shun her. Therefore, he is more than anxious to follow his master's command and bewitch this Athenian "lack-love."

This is the beginning of the turn-about twists that compose this madcap midsummer madness—all due to the magic of the pansy nectar and a quarrel between unseen sprites from another world. Significantly in this scene before Lysander falls asleep, he turns to Hermia and, with fervency, bids her goodnight, wishing sleep for them both, and wishing that "the wisher's eyes be pressed." His wish is ironic and foreboding. It presages exactly what is to happen within minutes. No sooner is he asleep than Puck enters and presses the magical juice on Lysander's closed eyelids; when he awakens, he will be transformed.

Puck has no sooner exited than Demetrius and Helena run on stage. Here is the real "lack-love." And no sooner is Demetrius on stage than he exits, running, leaving behind the panting, breathless Helena alone. Her breathlessness, however, does not stop her from uttering a rather long speech, laced with irony. "Happy is Hermia, wheresoe'er she lies" is her first reflection. Hermia, by coincidence, lies very near Helena. And Hermia will very soon be very unhappy and will exit running in hopeless confusion—exactly the same emotion and exactly the same way that Helena entered this scene.

Here, Helena reminds us of the lovesick Lysander. She bemoans her fate as a lover who can get no satisfaction. Bears bound away at her approach—just as does Demetrius. She envies Hermia's starry eyes, which seem to enchant men. Here again, note Shakespeare's emphasis on the *eyes*, for this play will have a good deal of fun with the serious matter of appearance and reality, distorted by the way people see things differently, especially after their eyes have been bewitched by the mischievous Puck.

After Helena has delivered her monologue filled with self-pity— a monologue that Shakespeare fills with exaggeration and mock romanticism to enhance the comic effect of her finding—by sheer coincidence—the model lover, the lover of her best friend, lying before her. Melodramatically, she entreats fate that he be merely sleeping and not dead. This is the epitome of Shakespeare's masterful comic technique in this play: Lysander is exactly the kind of lover who Helena wishes Demetrius to be. Here is coincidence coupled with the frustration and agony of unrequited love—all colored with witty hyperbole.

Moreover, when Lysander awakens, he delivers more of the same bombast. His speech is a tempestuous, boasting exclamation of praise for Helena, one that the audience is quick to recognize as being one of Shakespeare's first-rate comic effects. Promising to run through fire for Helena's "sweet sake," Lysander sighs passionately, "Transparent Helena!" Lysander means that he can see her love-filled heart, though she is clothed in flesh and a gown. But we, the audience, are alert to the clever juxtaposition between what is actually meant and what we see to be the truth of the matter. The truth is that Helena *is* transparent. Helena is a simple, hopeless

romantic—a real contrast to the realistic Hermia. Now that
Lysander is bewitched, he becomes as transparently a romantic as
Helena. He cannot wait to slay Demetrius (Helena's true love)—all
because of his newly awakened "love" for Helena. His over-blown
declarations of love end the scene between him and Helena as he em-
phasizes that his passion for Helena is "reasonable." Here again is
effective, extravagant comedy. Lysander is convinced that he loves
Helena because of reason ("reason says that you are the worthier
maid," he says, and moments later, he "reasons" that he "was till
now ripe not to reason," and, in conclusion, "reason becomes the
Marshall to my will"). Clearly the audience knows that Lysander is
not reasonable; he is intoxicated with the illusion of love, caused by
the magical nectar which Puck pressed on his eyelids. Reason has
absolutely nothing to do with Lysander's avowals of love. Puck's
magic potion was effective. Lysander's romantic metamorphosis is
floridly outrageous. The very sight of the sleeping Hermia sickens
his stomach; he suffers "the deepest loathing" for this woman
whom, only moments earlier, he spoke of lovingly as he envisioned
their two hearts knitted into one and their two bosoms interchained;
he uttered a "fair prayer" that he would "end life" when he would
"end loyalty" to Hermia. All has changed.

When Hermia awakens, she is alone on the stage and her
realistic terror as she awakens from a nightmare is genuine when
one compares it to the amplified intensity of love that we have just
heard.

This is dramatically a most effective contrast. And ironically,
she despairs at waking from a nightmare and finding Lysander
gone; Lysander, as she knows him, is indeed "gone." For a while, he
will be no more, and if Hermia thinks that she has awakened from a
nightmare, she is soon to realize that this midsummer-night will be a
very real nightmare for her before it is over.

ACT III—SCENE 1

Summary

Back in the glade where Titania lies sleeping, the rehearsal of
"Pyramus and Thisby" by Peter Quince and company runs into

trouble. No sooner is the rehearsal begun than Bottom interrupts with misgivings about the action of the play. The ladies in the audience will be frightened, he fears, when he, as Pyramus, draws a sword and kills himself. Snout agrees, and so does Starveling, who thinks they had better leave the suicide out. But Bottom has a better idea: let Quince write a prologue assuring the audience that Pyramus is only *Bottom* and that he does not really kill himself. Quince, to oblige his leading man, consents to add the prologue.

Then Snout has a problem: he is afraid that the Lion will frighten the ladies. Bottom agrees. And when Snout suggests that yet one more prologue be added, explaining that the Lion is not *really* a lion, Bottom comes up with a better idea: let half of Snug's face show through the lion's skin, and let Snug himself reassure the ladies that all will be safe. To this Quince also agrees, but he raises the first really practical question about the production: how are they going to present a sense of moonlight, by which Pyramus and Thisby meet? Bottom wonders whether the actual moon will shine on the night of the performance. "Look in the almanac," he urges, "find out moonshine!" Quince discovers that there *will* be a moon, but with a director's eye for stage effects, he suggests that Starveling, originally cast as Thisby's mother, should impersonate Moonshine, carrying a thornbush, which many Elizabethans believed the man in the moon to be carrying, and a lantern as a symbol of the moonlight itself. Quince also says that since Pyramus and Thisby talk through a chink in the wall between their two houses, there *must* be a wall. Snout, originally cast as Pyramus' father, says he doesn't "feel" the part, so Bottom sees possibilities: Snout can be the Wall; his clothes can be smeared with plaster, and he can make a chink with his fingers for the lovers to talk through.

As the rehearsal starts, Puck enters unseen and listens awhile, plotting more mischief. Bottom makes an exit behind some undergrowth, and Puck follows him. While Thisby (that is, Flute) is garbling "her" speeches, Puck transforms Bottom's round, chubby head into that of an ass with a grinning long countenance and long, hairy ears, and leads him in to speak his tender lines to Thisby. Quince, terrified, yells that the place is haunted, and everyone vanishes—except Bottom, the only one of the company left on stage.

Puck, invisible and inaudible to Bottom, goes after the fearful actors to have some more fun by misleading them and using different voices. Bottom, completely unaware of his transformation, thinks his fellow actors are playing a trick to scare him and grumbles undaunted when one after another of the troupe peeks timidly from the bushes and exclaims at his ass-head. To show that he is not afraid, Bottom walks up and down and sings in a rumbling bass. This awakens Titania, who with the magic juice on her eyes, sees him as a gentleman, one wise and handsome, and she instantly falls in love with him. She appoints four tiny fairies to attend him and lead him to her bower. Bottom takes it all in stride. He has such a good opinion of himself that nothing—absolutely nothing—surprises him.

Commentary

First off in this scene, one should remember that the lovely, enchanted Titania is sleeping, unbeknownst to Peter Quince and his troupe of amateur actors. She will awaken toward the end of the scene, but her sleeping, regal presence will be in constant, ever-present contrast to the buffoonery that comprises most of the action. After the light-hearted romantic entanglements and semi-serious throes of love in the previous scene, here is a recess. This is slapstick comedy, for as Shakespeare says in the stage directions *"Enter the clowns."*

As we have seen before, coincidence plays a key role in this broadly humorous subplot; immediately, Quince says that this is "a marvellous convenient place for our rehearsal." This could never happen in real life—only here, in the fanciful world of fairyland on Midsummer-Night's Eve, a moonlight evening created by Shakespeare to amuse and entertain us. There are no weighty messages—only foibles meant to help us laugh at ourselves.

As usual, when the scene opens, Bottom is taking over the role of director from Quince. He objects to certain things in "this comedy" that will never please the royal couple—in particular, things that might offend the ladies present. Remember: this "comedy" is, in reality, no comedy at all. It deals with the tragic deaths of Pyramus and Thisby. The *comedy* is contained in the antics of the amateur actors and their dead seriousness about the production. Bottom fears that his death scene may be too realistic for the ladies. Nothing could be further from the truth; the idea of Bottom transforming himself into an actor so consummate that he could cause fear and trembling when he draws his sword to commit suicide is amusingly preposterous. The simple Snout and even Starveling, however, are convinced that the ladies in the audience might be set to trembling by the super-reality of the production. Bottom obviously convinces *them*, even if he doesn't convince us. Bottom, to us, is a clown, a harmless show-off, but to his fellow actors, he is a figure of authority, even more so than Quince, the real director, and Bottom wants a prologue which will leave no doubt that the audience is witnessing only a play, *not* a slice-of-life production. And once Bottom has Quince's promise of a new prologue, he ponders yet another problem which he feels might sabotage the success of the play: the lion. The "ladies" might not to able to stand the ferocity of such a beast. Snug, it seems, must have mastered his part. Originally, he was afraid that he might not to able to do justice to the role. Now Snout insists on there being a prologue explaining that the lion is not *real*. And as added insurance against any of the ladies' delicate sensibilities being offended, Bottom suggests that at least half of Snout's face show through the lion's costume, in addition to a curtain speech by Snug, making sure that the audience knows that he is only *impersonating* a lion. This is yet one more example of Bottom's over-zealous concern for the production being a superb drama—in good taste, with only a modicum of violence. Such comedy, besides being appealing to the audience because of the incongruity of Bottom's logic was, no doubt, a great deal of fun for the actors who almost certainly worried and quibbled over just such trivial matters before a production was finally presented to the public. It is, however, Bottom's harmless, overstated, ever-interrupting self-importance which is the key to the humor in this scene.

Only Quince senses a real problem concerning the production of this "most lamentable comedy," and it is a problem that Shakespeare himself had to deal with and solve to give the light, romantic main plot the right amount of "spectacle"—that is, Shakespeare had to constantly make subtle references to the moon and to moonlight. He had to be absolutely sure that the audience was *always* aware that everything that they were seeing in these sections was happening at night, under the light of the magic midsummer-night's moon. Quince has a similar problem: *his* play takes place at night, and he is afraid that a mere actor portraying

Moonshine will not be sufficient for the theatrical sense he wants to achieve. Luckily, however, the moon is scheduled to shine that night, and Quince proposes that his actor carry a lantern so that the audience will be visibly reminded that the play is played at night, under a full moon. Then, when a suitable "Wall" is cast, and a chink conceived, made of spread fingers, all of the technical difficulties of the drama seem to be solved. The first rehearsal begins.

As it does, Puck enters, intent on more mischief. He provides the wit of this scene; the bumpkins provide the slapstick. Puck is tickled to find this motley lot of crude actors stumbling over their lines and over their entrances—and all this taking place next to the "hempken home-spun cradle" of the Fairy Queen. His innovative prank-playing is irrepressible, and he exits in a wink, re-entering with Bottom, as the latter enters with an ass's head in place of his own. Bottom, of course, doesn't realize that the transformation has taken place. Here, one must envision the "hero" of this play—Pyramus—making his entrance with a real ass's head in place of his own, declaiming to the dubiously beautiful Thisby that "If I were fair, Thisby, I were only thine."

Exit the Clowns. Ass-headed Bottom has scared his unlearned country friends half out of their wits. This night is suspect, anyway, for those who are naturally superstitious and when they see Bottom, they flee in genuine panic. Only when they have recovered from their shock do they reappear, for a minute, for one quick peek at the grotesque creature that sounds like Bottom, that acts like Bottom, but is more Ass than Bottom.

Bottom doesn't fully understand what has happened; hence, his punning that he will *not* be made an ass of. And it is while he is singing a nonsensical song to bolster his confusion and uncertainty that he chances to awaken the sleeping Titania; he twitters—first, like an "ousel cock" and then like a "throstle." Titania's drowsy response to Bottom's falsetto squawkings has become a stock source of laughter for all absurd situations: "What angel wakes me from my flowery bed?" Angel, indeed! It is the ass-headed Bottom, and the line no doubt received the same sure-fire laughter then that it does in today's productions. Titania is absolutely bewitched. The beautiful Queen of the Fairies beseeches the monstrous "gentle mortal" to sing more; she is "enthralled to thy shape," and she swears love for him. Oberon's plan is working. This is the "vile thing" he hoped would awaken her. Of course, Bottom is not really vile, but he certainly is outlandish. Yet one should not discount him entirely as a figure of comedy, for he is touched by Titania's loveliness and by her amorous attitude toward him. Doubtless he has never been so complimented, and thus he says, in rare understatement for him, "reason and love keep little company together now-a-days." This recalls Lysander's swearing that reason was the basis for his "love" for Helena. Bottom, then, is no longer the simple butt of Puck's joke. He wants to leave these woods. But Titania detains him, promising him wealth and a "purging of his mortal" state. She bewitches him with her loveliness and asks her fairy attendants to treat him royally and to hail him as their master. Seemingly, there is nothing Titania would not do for her beloved Bottom. Her praise for him is exquisite, ethereal poetry, jarringly inconsistent with Bottom's grotesque appearance.

Seemingly, Bottom finally comes to believe in Titania's declarations of passion for him. They exit, headed for Titania's bower and her reference to the moon before they exit (the moon being a symbol of chastity) is reinforced by another reference which she makes to a little flower "lamenting some enforced chastity." Obviously Titania and her new consort will soon consummate her desire—no enforced chastity for her—but they will not consummate their union until one of Titania's attendants complies and "ties up my lover's tongue." This witty exit line of Titania's saves the scene from being too grotesque. Titania *is* in love with Bottom, but he *does* seem to prattle on and on and on . . . .

ACT III—SCENE 2

Summary

Meeting Oberon in another part of the wood, Puck gives him a report of his various pranks. He has broken up the rehearsal of the play that Quince and his band of amateurs were preparing for Theseus' wedding and, moreover, he has scattered the actors in all directions throughout the forest and, most ingenious of all, he has changed Bottom into a man with an ass's head. Then Puck reveals his best achievement; he has caused Titania to fall in love with the ass-headed Bottom!

These magical pranks have worked out far better than Oberon ever anticipated, but he asks Puck if he succeeded in finding the Athenian youth. Puck proudly boasts that he has, and he says that he anointed his eyes so that when he awakened, the first thing he would see would be the girl sleeping near him and he would fall in love with her.

Oberon and Puck then hide as Demetrius and Hermia enter. Oberon immediately recognizes Demetrius as the disdainful lover, and to his dismay realizes that Puck has made a mistake: he bewitched the wrong Athenian youth! When he bewitched *Lysander's* eyes, it was Hermia who was sleeping "farther off," and here she is with a different Athenian. Their bitter speeches reveal that something has gone awry, but they do not know *what* or *how*. In fact, while Hermia was seeking her Lysander, she met Demetrius instead. He, of course, renews his amorous suit and, Hermia, of course, repulses him. Worse, she suspects that Demetrius has slain Lysander and hidden the body; otherwise, why was Lysander gone when she awoke? Repelled by Demetrius' grim appearance, she accuses him of murder. He retorts that *yes*, he probably looks dead because Hermia's stern cruelty has pierced his heart. Frantically, Hermia demands that Demetrius confess his crime, but he insists that to his best knowledge, Lysander is alive. Demetrius hopefully asks what reward he may expect if he can prove that Lysander is well, but Hermia spurns him and dashes off into the forest. Sorrowful and weary, Demetrius sinks down and falls asleep.

Oberon sharply chides Puck for having bewitched the eyes of a *true* lover rather than those of a "lack-love," a disdainful, coldhearted man. Then he bids Puck to seek out Helena and bring her to him. Obediently, Puck flits away, and Oberon drops the juice of the purple flower on Demetrius' eyes and pronounces a spell which will restore the love he once had for Helena.

Puck returns at once and says that he has found Helena nearby and that he heard Lysander pleading for her love. Philosophically, Puck declares "Lord, what fools these mortals be." Then he and Oberon stand out of sight as Lysander and Helena enter, Puck grinning at the thought that Helena, who formerly had no suitors, will now have two. And so it turns out. Lysander has hardly had time to woo her further—or she to reject his pleas as mockery, since she feels that he *really* loves Hermia—when Demetrius, whom Helena loves in vain (she thinks), suddenly appears and tries to kiss her hand. Since he has recently shown her nothing but rudeness, to be mocked by him now, of all times, is too much. She reproaches both him and Lysander bitterly, saying that she "knows" that they *both* love Hermia. But both men protest: they both truly love Helena, and when Lysander says that Demetrius can have Hermia, Demetrius says that Lysander can keep her. Thereupon Hermia, hearing Lysander's voice, comes in crying, "Why unkindly didst thou leave me so?" Lysander loses no time explaining: "For fair Helena," he says, adding that "the hate I bare thee made me leave thee." Hermia is crushed and incredulous.

Helena now thinks that even her dearest friend has joined with the men to mock her, and she rails at them for their ridicule of her. But Lysander rejects Hermia quite as rudely as Demetrius had Helena, and Hermia, at last convinced, blames Helena for stealing Lysander. Helena, though naturally gentle, is so annoyed that she calls Hermia a puppet, meaning that she is playing a part which Lysander and Demetrius have devised for her. But Hermia thinks that her tall, blonde friend has been making fun of her short stature. A quarrel ensues in which Hermia, a spitfire, would have scratched Helena and pulled her hair, except that Helena is timid and backs away, as both young men come to protect her. In so doing, however, they antagonize one another, and Lysander challenges Demetrius to a duel. They go out to find a suitable place, and once more Hermia blames Helena for the whole fracas. Helena, who knows her friend's fierceness of old, decides to flee. Looking after her, Hermia suddenly is bewildered and knows "not what to say."

All the while, of course, Oberon and Puck have been listening, and Oberon now blames Puck for all these mistakes; he thinks that there has been too much deliberate mischief-making. But Puck swears that it was a genuine mistake, though he admits he is not sorry, since he has thoroughly enjoyed the mortals' squabbles. In any case, Oberon now decides to set things right both in fairyland and on earth. He orders Puck to lead Lysander and Demetrius around and about through the woods, as he did with the actors; then he wants him to anoint Lysander's eyes with an herb which will remove the spell, so that all four lovers will return to Athens, uncertain whether the troubles of the night have been real or only dreams.

Oberon, meanwhile, will get Titania to give him the Indian boy and will release her from her infatuation with the ass-headed Bottom. Puck agrees, but he warns that all must be done quickly for it is nearly morning.

It is done quickly, and Puck taunts Lysander in Demetrius' voice, and Demetrius in Lysander's, until both are exhausted by futilely rushing about in the dark and finally fall asleep in the glade where Oberon and Puck had been standing when the scene began. Guided by Puck, Hermia and Helena come there too and fall asleep without seeing the young men. Then Puck anoints Lysander's eyes with the dispelling herb and predicts that when they awaken, all their troubles will be over.

Commentary

Oberon's first speech in this scene reveals his morbid interest in what has happened to Titania. His last wish, before he left her, was that "some vile thing" would awaken her; he wonders if she has awakened by now and what "she must dote on in extremity." Oberon's attitude here approaches imperiousness; his self-importance has become petty and his delight is extremely self-centered. Luckily, he does not have long to gloat, for Puck appears and satisfies his master's meddling curiosity: Titania is "with a monster in love," Puck reports, and in a long monologue, he describes in detail how he not only worked his sorcery on Titania, but how he played practical jokes on Quince and his friends, "leading them on in distracted fear" through briars and thorns, crying "Murder!" Puck revels in all that he has done. His speeches are the essence of self-congratulation: he chose the hero of the "play" which the country bumpkins were rehearsing, "Pyramus and Thisby," and, as it turned out, Pyramus turned out to be a real yokel, the "shallowest thickskin of that barren sort"; Puck thinks it was a fabulous stroke of good luck that he was able to transform *the* dolt of the acting troupe into the ass-headed lover of Titania. Oberon agrees; he could not be more pleased.

The devil-may-care Puck doesn't care at all when Oberon shows him that the wrong Athenian youth was enchanted by the magical pansy potion. Puck blames that on fate. Oberon, in contrast, is terribly upset by what has happened. He never intended to pervert true love and clearly he has; now he would like to right all wrongs except, for a while longer, the spell under which Titania is suffering. Yet despite all of Oberon's attempts to undo Puck's mischief, for most of this scene, we see the results of Puck's careless subterfuge. Our sympathy goes out to Helena. Very tall and very blonde and very pretty, Helena is also very simple. She is visibly a figure of despair, especially in this act. She has absolutely no clue as to what has happened. First, she was jilted and now her best friend's lover swears that *he* loves her—and her only—calling her his "dove" and referring to his old love, Hermia, as a "raven." Helena simply cannot fathom the enigmas of sexual love, much less the complexities of Puck's sorcery.

In contrast, even though Hermia is not aware of Puck's tricks, she is not reduced to despair. But she is certainly plagued once more by Demetrius' fawnings and, more important, she is terribly afraid that he has "slain Lysander in his sleep." She's convinced that he well might be a murderer and she is, therefore, infuriated when he begins to unravel a long chain of puns that proclaim, in effect, that it is not *he*, but *she*, who is the true murderer, for she murders with her fierce eyes, her eyes which "pierce the heart." She loses her temper and screams. She may be a tiny woman, but she does have a venomous tongue and a fierce temper. She detests Demetrius and his insipid wooings. And even if he can prove to her that Lysander is alive, she never wants to see Demetrius again.

All of this is part of the play's comedy, of course; one must not take these lovers' temper tantrums too seriously, just as one must not take too seriously Puck's perverse delight when he arranges for Lysander and Helena to be present when Demetrius (now "charmed" by Oberon to fall in love with Helena) is awakened by Helena's and Lysander's loud voices.

Puck is delirious to see how passionately "these mortals" treat their lovers, their lost lovers, their confused lovers, and the charade of love, in general. He has absolutely no sympathy for Helena's feeling that she has been exploited by "a manly enterprise." All for love, these two Athenian youths are ready to do battle and would if Hermia didn't happen on the scene and find herself also condemned by Helena. Like Puck, Hermia finds this fracas to be full of nonsense; but unlike Puck, she can see no humor in the situation. She surprises us by physically holding Lysander, despite his calling her all sorts of abusive names. Hermia weakens and releases him only after Lysander hints violence toward her. Unlike the hysterical Helena, she tries to bring reason into this chaos, and even while Lysander is cursing her as an Ethiopian (a jibe at her dark complexion), she refuses to believe that he seriously loves Helena. Only when he becomes dangerous does she turn dangerous and would have scratched Helena's eyes out if the men had not separated the two women. Thus we have two *men* itching to fight, and two *women* ready to unleash their tempers—all because of Oberon's magical nectar which he entrusted to the untrustworthy Puck to administer. The battle ensues as they all rush off stage—the men with their swords drawn and the diminutive Hermia, who has been called a dwarf, a vixen, and an acorn, hot on the heels of the long-legged "painted Maypole" Helena.

With the lovers gone, Oberon's anger reappears, but Puck is indifferent. This is great sport for him, but he will, if he must, envelope the woods in a great fog so that the angry lovers will not be able to do any real damage to one another and, after they are tired, the magic potion, now correctly applied, will restore lover to lover and will also release Titania from her infatuation with the ass-headed Bottom.

ACT IV—SCENE 1

Summary

Into this glade that Puck flooded with fog so that the lovers would dash blindly about until they fell asleep, Titania and the ass-headed Bottom and their attendants now enter. They do not notice the four young lovers sleeping there, and this is a fact which puzzles Titania later. (Shakespeare never explains this, but most commentators believe that this puzzling matter is a trifling oversight; perhaps Oberon, who is just behind them, wills it so.) Titania is still infatuated with Bottom, and she is crowning him with flowers and kissing his long, hairy ears. Bottom is unresponsive to her caresses, but he does enjoy having his "personal staff" scratch his head and bring him honey. At Titania's suggestion that perhaps he might enjoy some music, he asks not for a song by the fairies but for the clang and clatter of the triangle and bones. His taste in food is equally gross: a swatch of hay. Then suddenly he feels drowsy, and Titania sends the fairies away and enfolds him in her arms, and they sleep.

Oberon now comes forward and explains to Puck, who has appeared, that he has talked with Titania and she is willing to give up the Indian boy. Her excessive doting on Bottom, however, has made Oberon pity her, and so he disenchants Titania and bids Puck return Bottom to his human shape. Titania wakes and looks with surprise and loathing at Bottom. Oberon proposes that they dance in the palace at midnight to bless Theseus' marriage, and to lull the sleepers, they also dance on the grass to soft music. As the morning lark begins to sing, all the fairies exit.

In the distance, the sound of a hunting horn is heard, and Theseus, Hippolyta, Egeus, and the whole Athenian court enter on their way to a mountain top to watch the hunt and enjoy the music of the hounds re-echoed in the valley below. Theseus sees the sleeping girls, and Egeus identifies them and also the boys. Theseus now remembers that this is the day on which Hermia is to make her decision about her marriage to Demetrius. At Theseus' command, a huntsman wakens the lovers with his horn, and they kneel to Theseus. He bids them stand and tell him how they all came to be lying there together like *friends*. Lysander answers, but vaguely. Egeus demands judgment on him for attempting to block Hermia's marriage to Demetrius. But Demetrius, whose enchantment has rekindled his original love for Helena, now openly declares his love for only Helena. Theseus over-rules Egeus, abandons the hunt, and ordains that the two couples shall join with him and Hippolyta in a triple wedding. The court then withdraws toward Athens with the lovers following, their memories of the night still confused.

Meanwhile, Bottom awakens. He thinks that he is still at the rehearsal, waiting to answer his next cue (III.i.95). When he sees that the company is gone, he dimly recalls that he had a vision, though what it was he cannot quite remember. Practical as always, he gives it up, but resolves to have Peter Quince write him a ballad about it which he can use to pad his part in the play by singing it after Thisby's death. Then he shuffles out in search of his fellow actors.

Commentary

This scene is reminiscent of the scene in which Titania was sleeping while the country bumpkins were rehearsing and rewriting their "most lamentable" wedding play. Now the four lovers are asleep while the stage is filled with Bottom and his impromptu antics, the cavorting fairies, and finally, Theseus, Hippolyta, Egeus, and the attendants of the Athenian court. We know already that Oberon plans to unite the lovers in a perfect pairing, but Shakespeare extends the comedy for us a bit longer. The creation of the ass-headed Bottom is a brilliant stroke of dramatic spectacle and the sight of the lovely Queen of the Fairies waxing poetic and making romantic overtures make wonderful comedy. She utters lavish compliments that only the most ridiculous of stock lovers would declare; she praises his "amiable cheeks," adorns his head with musk roses, and kisses his "fair large ears"—to her, "a gentle joy." The incongruity of this Beauty and the Beast idyll is a monumental touch of genius.

And lest we forget that the ass-headed figure is still Bottom, the bumpkin, Shakespeare sustains his comedy by expanding on Bottom's already-established bossiness. His ass's head gives visual exaggeration to the bluster and grandiloquence that epitomized his relationship with the amateur actors and his obsession for being stage-center. Certainly he is literally at stage-center as he commands the fairy Peaseblossom to scratch his head and as he sends off another fairy, Cobweb, to kill a "red-hipp'd bumble-bee" so that he might have some fresh honey to dine on. He has assumed a proper consort's role, and the Queen is so enamored of him that her band of attendants dare not refuse him anything.

Oberon, who has witnessed this fanciful lunacy, welcomes Puck, and here we have evidence that this fanciful prank-playing of his is not as "villainous" as it once seemed to be; now he pities his queen whom Puck has made a fool of. When Puck details and recounts the "sweet favours" which she has done for the half-beast half-man, this recital obviously touches him. His answer to Puck contains an element of shame and guilt; the magic sorcery has been prolonged too long. After all, he does have the little Indian boy now. And logically in a comedy, there is a fine line between sustaining mockery for fun and for maliciousness. For Shakespeare to have continued Oberon's bewitchment of Titania would have spoiled the sense of joy which is the fabric of the play. Even Oberon now sees the ass-headed Bottom as a "hateful imperfection." Now he would "repair . . . this night's accidents." His wish is that all that has happened will ultimately be no more important than a dream—the dream of the play's title. Once again, we are reminded that all this action is happening at night, that all its dramatic histrionics have been as insubstantial as gossamer; this will finally be no more than a dream—for Lysander, Hermia, Demetrius, Helena, Bottom, and Titania.

Truly, Titania believes that all that has happened was only a dream—a vision, she calls it—until Oberon shares his secret with her that *he* was responsible for not only her enchantment, but for Bottom's transformation. The music that Titania's attendants provide lighten the mood and prepare us for the final scene of celebration.

The sleep is unraveled, and even Titania and Oberon seem to be reconciled, for Oberon says ". . . thou and I are new in amity." This midsummer-night is almost at an end as Puck hears the morning lark. The union of Theseus and Hippolyta promises to be blessed by the rulers of the fairy kingdom. The moon and the magic that have illuminated the play with illusion will soon be vanished as Puck, Titania, and Oberon leave "in . . . flight . . . swifter than the wandering moon."

The entrance of the mortals creates an entirely different mood. Daybreak is obvious for the audience; the royal hunt is on, and Theseus is anxious to reach the mountain top and, once there with his bride-to-be, he longs to exult in the echoes of the baying hunting hounds. The loveliness of the fairies' lullabies is an abrupt contrast to Hippolyta's remembering her own joy when she thrilled to the "musical . . . discord" of hunting hounds; "sweet thunder," she calls it. Shakespeare is pulling us back, bringing us back to reality. Dawn has broken the mood that was so carefully woven and sustained throughout these moon-lit acts that we actually came to believe in Oberon, to be concerned with Titania's fate, and pity the ass-headed Bottom, spoiled though he was by the fairy queen's affections. Now the long, drooping ears of the baying hunting hounds that "sweep away the morning dew" have replaced Bottom's enchanted, musk-rose garlanded "long and hairy ears."

But all is not sweetness and light—not yet. The gentle mood of the lovers, the mortal lovers, is broken when Egeus discovers his daughter lying with Lysander, and we recall here his fury and denunciation in the play's first scene. But his confusion in this scene makes him a comic figure of fun for he cannot understand Demetrius' and Helena's lying with his daughter and Lysander. His lines are short and suggest bewildered sputtering. Finally in this scene, Theseus fully attains his rightful stature, and he recognizes that "gentle concord" which exists between these young people and this, above all, is the most important factor at this moment.

Lysander, of course, is "half sleep, half waking" and confesses his intent to elope with Hermia beyond "the peril of the Athenian law." Egeus' anger is impotent against Demetrius' confession that his infatuation for Hermia is "melted as is the snow." Lovers they are all—except for the incensed Egeus, and so it is that Theseus decrees that *his* word is law and that the couples "shall eternally be knit," an image Lysander used when first he wished to bed down near Hermia.

The lovers, alone, ponder the night's "dream" as the scene ends, and it closes on a rattling, prattling monologue by Bottom, a gem of slapstick comedy intended to set us laughing once more. Seemingly, he utters broken fragments of nonsense, but Shakespeare laces Bottom's speech with philosophical puns and irony. Puck has already noted what fools mortals are—especially lovers; now Bottom echoes that thought when he muses that "man is but an ass . . . a patched fool." Bottom leaves the stage in high spirits, enraptured with the thought of creating a ballet as the climax for the nuptial play which he and his cohorts will perform for Theseus and Hippolyta.

ACT IV—SCENE 2

Summary

Back in Athens, at Peter Quince's house, the bumpkin-craftsmen are in despair. Bottom is nowhere to be found, and without him their play cannot go on. Even though he was almost assuming the authority of the director, understudying all the roles—in short, doing everything but rewriting the play—his spirit of theatrical magnetism is sorely missing; Bottom is necessary for the play. With his irrepressible spontaniety, his wit, and his marvelous multiple voice, he is the only suitable Pyramus among all the artisans that have been collected to present the play.

When Snug comes in with news of the triple wedding that is planned, the gloom deepens. A suitable play for a simple royal wedding was a problem enough for them all; now their troubles are tripled. Theseus is known for his generosity; Bottom as Pyramus might have been awarded a pension, sixpence a day for life. What can be done now?

Then, to his friends' joy, Bottom appears with news that their play has been put on the "preferred list," and he exhorts them to check their costumes, remember their parts, and forgo all worries: the play must go on. And one more thing. As a last matter of prime importance for this performance, the actors must all swear to give up onions and garlic.

Commentary

This short scene returns us to the broad comic element in the play. The artisans, all of them serious amateurs, *must* complete preparations for their play, and Bottom, the star of the production, cannot be found. Amusing melodrama initiates the scene's mood: dismay is rampant. Starveling unknowingly furnishes us a droll laugh when he suggests that Bottom has probably been "transported." Bottom has indeed been "transported"—into the land of fairy magic, but soon he will return, and they will all be able to continue with the play.

It is pleasing to hear the other players' praise of Bottom. Flute is convinced that no one in Athens has a better sense of wit than Bottom, and Peter Quince, the director, is convinced that no one except Bottom can adequately perform the role of Pyramus because besides having an innate sense of theater, Bottom is the only one of the troupe who is handsome enough to be the hero. This is the second reference we have had concerning Bottom's good looks, a detail often neglected by critics, readers, and even directors of the play, and it is a detail which is noteworthy since Puck plays the cruelest trick of all on Bottom. Bottom's ridiculous ass's head is the visual focal point of the comedy.

The second section of this scene increases the anxiety of melodrama among the actors, for when Snug announces that the marriages have been performed, we now know that the court awaits the production of "Pyramus and Thisby." It *must* be presented—and Bottom is still missing. Yet because this is a comedy, mock melodrama, and a cliff-hanger situation, Bottom does appear—at the last possible moment. He is thoroughly his old self, assuming charge of everything. We cannot help but smile at his professional concern that the false beards be in readiness, that the actors attend to "new ribands to [their] pumps," and that everyone should give his part a final reading. By rights, this should be Quince's "role," but since the beginning of the play, Bottom has been stage-center. The play-within-a-play is about to begin, and Shakespeare combines jubilation and madcap madness throughout the final preparations for the denouement of his midsummer-night's entertainment.

ACT V—SCENE 1

Summary

At Theseus' palace, the three-fold marriage has been performed. Hippolyta wonders to her new husband about the strange story which the other two couples have told. He finds it all unbelievable since he knows that lovers, like lunatics and poets, have potent imaginations. Hippolyta observes that the two happily married couples prove, however, that *something* must have happened. The newlyweds then come in.

Theseus asks that Philostrate, Master of the Revels, reveal what entertainments have been proposed to shorten the hours until bedtime—when the nuptial unions can be consummated. Philostrate hands him a list. Three mythological shows are rejected as trite or unsuitable. The fourth is somewhat of an oddity: "Pyramus and Thisby." Theseus puzzles over the description of this play: how can it be funny and tragic, short and, he fears, boresome? Philostrate says that he saw it and shed tears of mirth over the ineptness of both the dialogue *and* the actors. When Theseus hears that unedu-cated, bumpkin-type workingmen have prepared it, the play's pro-duction is certain. This type of absurdity is too good to let pass. He says that he will hear it. Philostrate warns him that the only pleasure it can give will derive from the humble subjects' loyalty and the trouble they have taken to produce it. Theseus assures him that these are the very qualities which a good ruler enjoys most. He will hear the play. Hippolyta says that she dislikes seeing earnest failure, no matter *how* well-intended. But Theseus reminds her that a man's will and his intentions are far more important than his deeds; in fact, he trusts inarticulate service more than glib speeches.

With a flourish of trumpets, Quince enters and speaks his prologue; but he is so nervous that he halts in the middle of his sentence and conveys the opposite of his intended meaning. Theseus, Hippolyta, and Lysander make audible fun of this. But the show goes on. Quince introduces Pyramus, Thisby, the Wall, Moonshine, and the Lion, and gives a short synopsis of the plot, using old-fashioned alliterative verse in relating the climactic double suicide.

All now go out except Snout, the Wall, who tells what he is and, in addition, shows the finger-formed cranny through which the lovers will whisper their deep affection for one another. The courtiers agree that he speaks very well—for a wall. Bottom as Pyramus approaches the Wall, looks through the chink, and curses the Wall because he cannot see Thisby. When Theseus wonders aloud whether the Wall will curse back, Bottom steps out of his role to explain. No, no, he says. And that is Thisby's cue to enter. She and Pyramus talk through the chink but, alas, they cannot kiss, but they do agree to meet at old Ninny's tomb. They exit, and the Wall explains that his part is now done, and he exits also.

Hippolyta is embarrassed at such silly stuff, but Theseus remarks that even the best actors create only a brief illusion, and that the worst, like Quince and company, can be helped out by a sympathetic and imaginative audience.

Now Lion and Moonshine come on stage. Snug, as the Lion, duly reassures the hearers that he is only Snug and will *not* bite them. But he and Moonshine are too much for even Theseus' courtesy. Now the witticisms fly so thick and fast that Moonshine abandons his verse part and simply proclaims in prose that his lantern is the moon, he is the man in the moon, this thornbush is his thornbush, and this dog his dog. Hippolyta groans that she is tired of the Moon; she wishes that he would wane.

Thisby enters at old Ninny's tomb, but finds no Pyramus; the Lion roars and Thisby runs away, dropping her mantle, which the Lion tears and bloodies with the gore of some animal he has killed earlier. When the Lion goes out, Pyramus enters, thinks Thisby has been killed and eaten, stabs himself, and dies in operatic, oratorical fashion. Then Thisby returns, and finding her lover dead, stabs herself, and falls on his body. The suicides are carried out in a flurry of execrable old-fashioned verse and ironical commendation from the audience.

Bottom leaps up "from the dead" to ask if Theseus will hear the epilogue or see a rustic dance—which? Theseus can take no more. Declining to see the epilogue, he consents to watch the dance. When that is finished, the newly married couples at last retire for bed. Three epilogues to the whole play are supplied, however. The first is Puck's speech, a poetic description of the night, as he flits about, sweeping the palace with a broom; the second is Oberon's promised blessing of the house and the wedding beds, while the fairies dance and sing; the third, a conventional one, is an "apology" by Puck for the "weak and idle" drama. He asks the audience to applaud; he promises that the production will be far better next time.

Commentary

Primarily, the final scene of this comedy brings together the three pairs of lovers on stage. They are now married and they happily anticipate an evening's entertainment before their marriages are consummated. Harmony reigns, presided over by Theseus. Clearly, he is fond of "the poet's pen" and the dramatist's ability "to airy nothing/ A local habitation and a name." He admires strong imagination for it reveals "more than cool reason ever comprehends." He is the enlightened patron of the arts, a Renaissance man of appreciation, urging the lovers to enjoy the "mirth" of this entertainment "between our after-supper and bed-time." To Hippolyta, who is *not* fond of amateur theatricals, he urges forbearance and patience. These amateurs aim to please. Theseus has seen inexperienced actors before; they "shiver and look pale,/ Make periods in the midst of sentences,/ And throttle accents in their fears. . . . Trust me, sweet," he asks. His role is small in this play, but it is multidimensional. Earlier, we saw a young man's sexual yearning for his bride-to-be, then he was asked to decide Hermia's fate; now he instructs Hippolyta on how to enjoy the play. He is sure that it will probably be ineptly performed, but the spirit of joy and goodwill shared by all and extended to the actors is far more important than a critical stance. Besides being intelligent and spirited, Theseus is admirably generous.

The play "Pyramus and Thisby," which we finally see performed, is as absurdly comic as we expected it to be. Like many other Elizabethan plays, it opens with a prologue in which Quince *means* to say, most of all, that he and the actors will try to please the court. However, as Quince pronounces the prologue, he pauses at all the wrong places and, finally, what he says is the very opposite of what he means to say. Even Theseus is confused and, as we might expect, Hippolyta is reminded of a child tootling on a recorder.

As the prologue continues and the actors are introduced, there is a sense that Quince knows that his prologue is not going well, and so he improvises—between many commas—trying to salvage the motley appearance of the actors and their nervous confusion. "A tangled chain" is how the play is described—"nothing impaired, but all disordered."

To fully appreciate this play-within-a-play, we must recall Bottom's enthusiasm for his hero's role (no doubt a parody on Theseus' deeds) and the skinny Flute in a gown as the lovely Thisby. Bottom's speech is peppered with many O's of woe: there are three sighs of "O night," in addition to "O wall, O sweet, O lovely wall. . . . O wall, O sweet and lovely wall." To praise the wall that separates him and his beloved is incongruous, of course, but he soundly curses it within minutes when he realizes that he cannot spy Thisby through its chink.

At this point, there is much improvising between Pyramus and Theseus (and later by other members of the court). Theseus thinks that the wall should curse back. Pyramus disagrees; Thisby's cue is due any minute; thus Theseus should not fear: Thisby *will* appear—and, on the cue, "yonder she comes." Now Pyramus is able to "*hear* my Thisby's face" (italics mine). The vows of love which they exchange are some of Shakespeare's gems of intentional mispronounciation, but they, the lovers, continue their lines of love and do *try* to kiss through the finger-fashioned chink in the wall. This is fine comedy—for all except Hippolyta. To her, "This is the silliest stuff that ever I heard." Theseus, of course, realizes that this is *not* good drama, but he reminds Hippolyta in one of his most significant speeches that "imagination mends." He considers motives foremost, not performances *per se*.

Once again we should recall that when Lion and Moonshine enter, Snug (the Lion) had decided to have his head half out of the Lion's costume so that he wouldn't frighten the ladies of the court. Even Theseus comments on Snug's not seeming to be a threatening beast; on the contrary, Theseus thinks that Snug seems to be "a very gentle beast," and Demetrius picks up on Theseus' goodhearted jesting and remarks, "The very best at a beast, my lord, that e'er I saw."

The part of the Moon is gently jeered by the court, who all now seem to savor the earnest, but absurdly serious attempt of the actors to please. Moon forgets his lines, but it doesn't matter because the members of the audience are thoroughly enjoying themselves, and even Hippolyta becomes wryly clever when she says that perhaps the moon will wane.

When the lovers finally do rendezvous at Ninny's tomb, Snug roars so superbly that Thisby runs off stage. "Well roar'd, Lion," Demetrius cheers, and Theseus echoes, "Well run, Thisby." And even Hippolyta by now is laughing. "Well shone, Moon," she calls out.

Lion shakes Thisby's mantle in his mouth and exits, just as Pyramus enters and, all aglow with love, praises the "sweet moon" for its "sunny beams." But when he discovers Thisby's bloodied mantle, he breaks into a long, disjointed monologue of poor rhymes, malapropisms, absurd colloquialisms, and ridiculous high-blown rhetoric. Surely it is one of Shakespeare's best mock speeches of love's agony. It ends with these lines: "Quail, crush, conclude, and quell!" Thereupon, he stabs himself and dies—but not before great and prolonged deliberation. Bottom, as Pyramus, indulges in every theatrical trick he knows before he dies.

Thisby's lines are equal, almost, to Pyramus' absurdly anguished cries: she bewails his "lily lips, his cherry nose, his cowslip cheeks, and his eyes, as green as leeks." Then with a quick thrust of her sword, she too is dead.

Theseus' praise for the play is well deserved; it was fine entertainment. Perhaps it could have been improved, he half-heartedly suggests, if Pyramus had hanged himself with one of Thisby's garters. But no matter, it was all good fun. Thus he bids his "sweet friends, to bed . . . [for] nightly revels and new jollity."

Once again the fairies enter, led by Puck, and inhabit the world of the stage. Puck frolics much like a janitor, cleaning up the tag ends, and is joined in his dancing and singing by the happy Oberon, Titania, and their attendants. The married couples are blessed, as Oberon gives each fairy magical dew to consecrate the mortals' unions. Puck then bids the audience adieu.

CRITICAL ANALYSIS

THEME

The theme of *A Midsummer-Night's Dream* is that "love hath no law but his own," is blind, unreasonable and unpredictable; "all's fair in love and war." But since it is an entertaining fantasy, neither realistic nor tragic even for a moment, we must not take its romantic moments too seriously; in fact, we shall find that they are themselves made fun of, reflected in the distorting mirror of farce.

Practically everything that is said and done in the play is related to this theme, so that the whole is a network of parallel, circling, or crisscrossing threads which somehow form a satisfying pattern. Or, if we think of the parts separately, it is like a piece of music in which a single motif is repeated in different keys and tempos.

Theseus, though he loves Hippolyta and will wed her, has won her love doing her injuries. Hermia for love of Lysander defies her father and Athenian law. Demetrius makes love to Helena and then woos Hermia. Hermia, wooed by two young men who in the eyes of the world are indistinguishably handsome, rich, and well-born, dotes upon one and hardly knows that the other exists. Demetrius, who has courted Helena and eventually marries her, hates her for a time, is sick when he does look on her, and spurns her with his foot. She, for a few hours of his disdainful company, betrays the secret of her dearest friend.

We are not told whether or not the artisans have wives or sweethearts. They are obsessed by the dream of moving an audience with a tragedy on the theme of obsessive love.

Oberon and Titania, though they are lord and lady and eventually rejoin in amity, are jealous of one another over Oberon's straying after nymphs and admiring Hippolyta, and Titania's doting on Theseus to the point of helping him in his earlier love affairs with mortal women. Also Titania, though Oberon is her lord, had a priestess of her own and cherishes the priestess' boy; Oberon, though Titania is his lady, uses his magic to get the boy from her. Their quarrel is reflected in the unseasonable weather on earth and in the young lovers' quarrel which follows the transfer of Lysander's affection, and Titania's fondness for Bottom mirrors in ridiculous fashion the doting of Hermia and Helena and of all mortals who lavish affection on unworthy objects. Only the stability of the mature and noble Theseus, who does not believe in fairies and distrusts the excesses of lovers, introduces order into the pattern and brings all right in the end.

KINDS OF UNREALITY

We have said that the play is a fantasy, unreal. Its unreality is of several different kinds. The very title warns us that it is all a dream. And that is the impression which the young lovers and Bottom retain at the end. But just as Quince and his company put on a play-within-a-play, so Hermia, Titania, and Bottom have a dream-within-a-dream. Another unreality is that of time and place: it all happened a long time ago in a mythical city ruled by a mythical Duke and his equally mythical bride. The young lovers and the actors are closer to reality; yet we know even while we are laughing at them that never on earth have there been couples quite so fond and so confused, or comedians so uproariously inept. Moreover, both of these groups are touched by the supernatural world of the fairies. But to say that the play is a fantasy is not to say that it has no meaning. The characters under the influence of magic in the mazes of a dream do nothing that is actually impossible in life.

SETTING

The setting of *A Midsummer-Night's Dream* is that of a masque, the stately ancestor of our musical comedy, privately staged at some great house or palace, or at the Inns of Court and, like the musical comedy, at fabulous expense. Dancing, singing, elaborate costumes and spectacle were the elements of the masque. It was also receptive to the introduction of the supernatural and of burlesque clowning. Since the public playhouses of Shakespeare's time were financially unable to compete with private entertainments in scenes, machines, and costumes, he supplied instead, a setting of lovely poetic descriptions.

SOURCES

The term "sources" needs careful definition in its relation to the plays of Shakespeare. With the exception of Sir Thomas North's *Plutarch*, his sources are for the most part simply raw material. What he discarded is often as significant as what he kept. What he added is always vitalizing. But most important of all is the unification of the whole and its transmutation into high art.

Twentieth-century investigation of Shakespeare's sources has tended in ever-increasing measure to reveal the scope and variety of his reading, the speed with which he could select what was relevant to his purpose, and the retentiveness of his memory. A play so composite as *A Midsummer-Night's Dream* provides a striking example of these processes and qualities. The stories which comprise it are not found together in any previous work, so that the plot is in a very real sense original. The following attempt to examine separately the four stories involved—those of Theseus and Hippolyta, the young lovers, the fairies, and the actors and their interlude—throws into sharp relief the inventiveness with which they have been rounded out and the ingenuity with which they have been interwoven.

The Knight's Tale of Chaucer seems the most probable source for the "enveloping action," the story of Theseus and Hippolyta. Chaucer speaks of Theseus as the ruler of ancient Athens and gives him the title of Duke rather than King, as though Athens were an Italian city-state. He is the conqueror of the Amazons, whose Queen Hippolyta he has captured and wedded and he is celebrating the occasion by a great feast (I.i.19). Much is made of the observance of the rite of May and of the Duke's fondness for hunting with his hounds at that season.

Chaucer's main theme is the obsessive love of Palamon and Arcite, two young noblemen imprisoned by Theseus after his capture of the Amazons, for Emily (sister of Hippolyta) and the rupture of their friendship by that love. No similarity of names or characters can be adduced to indicate that Palamon, Arcite, and Emily suggested the young lovers in *A Midsummer-Night's Dream*; yet the situation is there in Chaucer, and the addition of a second girl to "square the triangle" is just what a dramatist would think of at once. Later in Chaucer's tale, Arcite is released from prison, re-enters Theseus' service incognito, and rises to be one of the Duke's favorite squires. He calls himself Philostrate.

The Hippolyta of the play owes nothing to any source except her presence as the betrothed of Theseus. She is more lightly sketched than any other mortal in the play except the minor actors. Certainly if we had not read of her in mythology we should never take her for an Amazon.

The *Life of Theseus* by Plutarch, in North's translation (1579) supplied Shakespeare with a few details. The name Egeus appears (as also in Chaucer), though as the father of Theseus, as a king and not merely a citizen of Athens. Plutarch has him consult the oracle at Delphi, and the answer is given by Apollo's "nun" (I.i.70). Plutarch mentions the admiration of Theseus for his kinsman Hercules (V.i.46-47). Versions of Theseus' affairs with Perigouna (II.i.78), Aegles (II.i.79), Ariadne, and Antiope (II.i.80) appear. His battle with the Centaurs (V.i.44-45) is also mentioned.

The important influence of North's *Plutarch* was on Shakespeare's conception of Theseus as a wise and generous ruler. Chaucer says that he was renowned for wisdom, but deals at length with him as a builder and as an arranger of tournaments. Of the two accounts of Theseus which Shakespeare used, North's *Plutarch* and Chaucer, the former is more likely to have fostered the picture of the great ruler. Probably also, Shakespeare's Theseus reflects Shakespeare's own ideal of kingship as exemplified in Henry V. And it is possible, too, that a compliment to some Elizabethan noble was intended.

Unless we admit the possibility that Shakespeare's young lovers were derived from Chaucer's Palamon, Arcite, and Emily, with the natural addition of a second girl, the quartet is Shakespeare's own addition to the cast of characters. The first possibility is far from negligible, but in any case it applies only to their positions as pieces in the game, not to their personalities. Shakespeare's four are freshly but lightly sketched, and the types are universal in

56

stories of romantic love, the boys externally indistinguishable, the girls sharply contrasted. Nevertheless, they carry the main story, speak the most lines, and draw from their creator much of the most memorable writing in the play (I.i), as well as its peak of high comedy (III.ii).

STUDY QUESTIONS

1. Egeus is the father of (a) Helena; (b) Hermia; (c) Titania.
2. Hermia is determined to marry (a) Demetrius; (b) Philostrate; (c) Lysander.
3. Hippolyta is Queen of the (a) Athenians; (b) Fairies; (c) Amazons.
4. The juice from Oberon's magic flower has the power to (a) put people to sleep; (b) make one fall in love with the first object one sees; (c) enable one to forget all about someone he or she loves.
5. Theseus tells Hermia that she must obey her father's will or die. The only alternative is (a) she will be exiled for life; (b) she will be abandoned in the woods; (c) she must take a vow of chastity and become a priestess.
6. The cause of the quarrel between Oberon and Titania is (a) rivalry for power; (b) a small Indian boy each wishes to keep; (c) Puck's meddling.
7. Oberon wishes to unite happily (a) Helena and Lysander; (b) Bottom and Titania; (c) Hermia and Lysander.
8. A buskin is (a) a sharp dagger; (b) a high shoe with raised soles; (c) a kind of elf.
9. Oberon directs Puck to anoint with magic juice the eyes of (a) Demetrius; (b) Hermia; (c) a disdainful youth.
10. The first person who meets Queen Titania's eyes when she awakens is (a) Oberon; (b) Bottom; (c) Puck.
11. Puck transforms Bottom (a) with the trunk and tusks of an elephant; (b) by reducing him to the size of an elf; (c) by giving him the head of an ass.
12. The four fairies in Titania's train are Cobweb, Moth, Mustard-seed, and (a) Butterfly; (b) Peaseblossom; (c) Sweetpea.
13. What physical characteristic of Hermia's is referred to during

the fight in the wood (a) pale face; (b) short stature; (c) somber expression?

14. Puck is also known as (a) Master of the Revels; (b) The Fairy King; (c) Robin Goodfellow.
15. When Bottom is tended by the fairies, he asks for music, a barber to shave him, and for (a) kidney pie; (b) strong ale; (c) pease and hay.
16. Oberon's reaction to Titania's enchanted attachment for the ass-headed Bottom is one of (a) scorn; (b) anger; (c) pity.
17. When Oberon and Titania are reconciled, all of the fairies and elves leave to attend (a) a ball at court; (b) Theseus' wedding feast; (c) a maypole dance.
18. When Theseus is told of the night's strange events, he decrees that (a) Hermia shall be put to death; (b) Hermia must marry Demetrius; (c) Hermia and Lysander and Helena and Demetrius shall be married at once.
19. "Pyramus and Thisby," the play presented by Bottom and his friends, is (a) a comic interlude; (b) a tragic playlet; (c) a most lamentable comedy.
20. When the parts are given out, Bottom wishes to play (a) the heroine; (b) the hero; (c) all of them.

ANSWERS: 1-b; 2-c; 3-c; 4-b; 5-c; 6-b; 7-a; 8-b; 9-c; 10-b; 11-c; 12-b; 13-b; 14-c; 15-c; 16-c; 17-b; 18-c; 19-c; 20-c.

BIBLIOGRAPHY

ADAMS, JOSEPH QUINCY. *A Life of William Shakespeare.* New York: Houghton-Mifflin Co., 1923.

ALEXANDER, PETER. *Shakespeare.* London: Oxford University Press, 1964.

BARBER, C. L. *Shakespeare's Festive Comedy.* Princeton: Princeton University Press, 1959.

BENTLEY, G. E. *Shakespeare, a Biographical Handbook.* Theobold Lewis, ed. New Haven: Yale University Press, 1961.

58

BETHELL, S. L. *Shakespeare and the Popular Tradition.* London: King and Staples, 1944.

BRIGGS, KATHERINE M. *The Anatomy of Puck.* London: Rutledge and Paul, 1959.

BROWN, JOHN RUSSELL. *Shakespeare and his Comedies.* London: Methuen and Co., 1957.

CHAMBERS, E. K., ed. *A Midsummer-Night's Dream* (The Arden Shakespeare). revised by Edith Rickert. Boston: D. C. Heath & Co., 1916.

CLEMEN, W. *The Development of Shakespeare's Imagery.* London: Methuen and Co., 1951.

CRAIG, HARDIN. *An Interpretation of Shakespeare.* New York: Dryden Press, 1948.

CRAIG, HARDIN, ed. *A Midsummer-Night's Dream in Shakespeare.* revised ed. New York: Scott, Foresman and Co., 1958.

DE LA MARE, WALTER. *"Introduction,"* in *A Midsummer-Night's Dream.* C. Aldred, ed. London: The Macmillan Company, 1935.

DORAN, MADELEINE, ed. *A Midsummer-Night's Dream* (The Pelican Shakespeare). Baltimore: Penguin Books, 1959.

ELLIS-FERMOR, UNA M. *Shakespeare the Dramatist.* London: Geoffrey Cumberlege, 1948.

FURNESS, HORACE HOWARD, ed. *A Midsummer-Night's Dream.* Philadelphia: Lippincott, 1895.

GODDARD, HAROLD C. *The Meaning of Shakespeare.* Chicago: University of Chicago Press, 1951.

KNIGHT, G. WILSON. *The Shakespearean Tempest.* London: Oxford University Press, 1932; reprinted New York: Barnes & Noble, Inc., 1960.

MUIR, KENNETH. "Pyramus and Thisbe: A Study in Method," in *Shakespeare Quarterly V.* New York: Shakespeare Association of America, 1954.

PALMER, JOHN. *Comic Characters of Shakespeare.* London: The Macmillan Company, 1946.

PARROTT, THOMAS MARC. *Shakespearean Comedy.* New York: Oxford University Press, 1949.

PRIESTLEY, J. B. *The English Comic Characters.* London: The Bodley Head, 1925; reprinted 1963.

PURDOM, C. B. *What Happens in Shakespeare.* London: John Baker, 1963.

SITWELL, EDITH. *A Notebook on William Shakespeare.* London: Oxford University Press, 1928.

WATKINS, RONALD. *Moonlight at the Globe.* London: Michael Joseph, 1946.

WELSFORD, ENID. *The Court Masque.* Cambridge: University Press, 1927.

WILSON, J. DOVER. *The Essential Shakespeare,* New York: Cambridge University Press, 1932.

NOTES

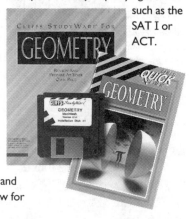